"So many Christian parents fall into do in the hearts of their children what only grace can accomplish. Armed with threats, manipulation, and guilt, they attempt to create change that only the cross of Jesus Christ makes possible. It is so encouraging to read a parenting book that points parents to the grace of the cross and shows them how to be instruments of that grace in the lives of their children."

Paul David Tripp, president of Paul Tripp Ministries

"This is not just a book on parenting; this is deep training in the gospel. Elyse Fitzpatrick shows parents how to model themselves after the heavenly Father, who changed his children not by wrath and the law but by grace. A lot of books talk about gospel-centeredness in theory; this book shows you how to apply it to one of life's most important relationships."

J. D. Greear, pastor of Summit Church and author of *Gospel*

"This book is about how we, as parents, must find our strength in God alone, and how our children need to be invited into that same gospel story. It is both humbling and encouraging, challenging and practical."

Rachel Joy Welcher, editor at *Fathom* magazine and author of *Talking Back to Purity Culture*

"Ten years ago, *Give Them Grace* was one of the pieces of parenting gold that helped me understand the gospel myself as a young mother. It stood in such contrast to heavy-handed Christian parental 'how-to' advice and instead it centered me on 'who to.' I am so excited this is rereleasing in a space with many loud voices. This will be a breath of fresh air to parents who want to center their parenting on the grace of Jesus Christ."

Jami Nato, author, mother of four, and entrepreneur

Give
Them
Grace

Other Books by the Authors

Elyse M. Fitzpatrick and Jessica Thompson

*Answering Your Kids' Toughest Questions: Helping Them
Understand Loss, Sin, Tragedies, and Other Hard Topics*

Elyse M. Fitzpatrick

Finding the Love of Jesus from Genesis to Revelation

*Home: How Heaven and the New Earth
Satisfy Our Deepest Longings*

Worthy: Celebrating the Value of Women
(with Eric M. Schumacher)

Jessica Thompson

*Everyday Grace: Infusing All Your Relationships
with the Love of Jesus*

Give Them Grace

Leading Your Kids to Joy and Freedom through Gospel-Centered Parenting

Elyse M. Fitzpatrick and Jessica Thompson

Revell

a division of Baker Publishing Group
Grand Rapids, Michigan

© 2011, 2024 by Elyse M. Fitzpatrick and Jessica L. Thompson

Published by Revell
a division of Baker Publishing Group
Grand Rapids, Michigan
RevellBooks.com

Printed in the United States of America

Library of Congress Cataloging-in-Publication Data
Names: Fitzpatrick, Elyse, 1950– author. | Thompson, Jessica, 1975– author.
Title: Give them grace : leading your kids to joy and freedom through gospel-centered parenting / Elyse M. Fitzpatrick and Jessica Thompson.
Description: Grand Rapids, Michigan : Revell, a division of Baker Publishing Group, [2024] | Includes bibliographical references.
Identifiers: LCCN 2024003936 | ISBN 9780800746179 (paper) | ISBN 9780800746377 (casebound) | ISBN 9781493447169 (ebook)
Subjects: LCSH: Child rearing—Religious aspects—Christianity. | Law and gospel.
Classification: LCC BV4529 .F559 2024 | DDC 248.8/45—dc23/eng/20240224
LC record available at https://lccn.loc.gov/2024003936

Original edition published as *Give Them Grace: Dazzling Your Kids with the Love of Jesus* (Crossway, 2011).

Chapter 9 is adapted from *Jesus and Gender: Living as Sisters and Brothers in Christ* by Elyse M. Fitzpatrick and Eric M. Schumacher (Kirkdale, 2022).

Unless otherwise indicated, Scripture quotations are from the Holy Bible, New International Version®, NIV®. Copyright © 1973, 1978, 1984, 2011 by Biblica, Inc.® Used by permission of Zondervan. All rights reserved worldwide. www.zondervan.com. The "NIV" and "New International Version" are trademarks registered in the United States Patent and Trademark Office by Biblica, Inc.®

Scripture quotations labeled CSB are from the Christian Standard Bible®. Copyright © 2017 by Holman Bible Publishers. Used by permission. Christian Standard Bible® and CSB® are federally registered trademarks of Holman Bible Publishers.

Scripture quotations labeled ESV are from The Holy Bible, English Standard Version® (ESV®). Copyright © 2001 by Crossway, a publishing ministry of Good News Publishers. Used by permission. All rights reserved. ESV Text Edition: 2016

Scripture quotations labeled MSG are from *The Message*. Copyright © 1993, 2002, 2018 by Eugene H. Peterson. Used by permission of NavPress. All rights reserved. Represented by Tyndale House Publishers.

Scripture quotations labeled NLT are from the *Holy Bible*, New Living Translation. Copyright © 1996, 2004, 2015 by Tyndale House Foundation. Used by permission of Tyndale House Publishers, Carol Stream, Illinois 60188. All rights reserved.

All italics in Scripture quotations are the authors' emphasis.

Cover design by Laura Klynstra.

The authors are represented by the literary agency of The Gates Group.

Baker Publishing Group publications use paper produced from sustainable forestry practices and postconsumer waste whenever possible.

24 25 26 27 28 29 30   7 6 5 4 3 2 1

To all the faithful parents
who love their dear ones
and want them to love the Dear One
who gave his life for them.

Contents

Introduction

How Does Your Faith Inform Your Parenting?

So much has changed since the original edition of this book came out in May 2011—not just globally but also in our own lives. We have learned more. We have experienced more. We have grown. We now have a better understanding of what it means to care for the whole child. We've also become aware of some errors in the way we used to think and believe, which is why we are so grateful for the chance to update this book and add two new chapters— one regarding our children's anxiety and depression and another on gender. While much has changed for us, the most important things have stayed the same. Our desire for parents, children, grandparents, and caregivers to know the love of God in Christ is still the heartbeat of this book, and the primary question we still want to answer is, Does our faith inform our parenting?

As you will see, this isn't a method to guarantee your children's success or salvation. This is a way for you to find hope and healing in the gospel and to preach the gospel to yourself and your children as you seek to raise them in the instruction of the Lord. In addition, we are not asking you to follow us. We, like you and your children, are broken and need a Savior too. Whether we are

11

successful or not in our parenting does not change the power of the gospel message—that Jesus came to seek and save the lost. What matters most to us is that you experience the same grace you hope to give to your children.

A couple things to note: one, we recognize this book is written for parents of neurotypical children. If your child is neurodivergent, parts of this book will be helpful, but we hope you'll take what's helpful for your children to process the gospel and the world around them—and leave what isn't helpful, as you see fit. Two, if you become overwhelmed while reading this book, take your time. Know you can rest in God's grace for you and be safe and at home with him.

How Should a Christian Parent Respond?

Jessica heard a terrifying scream emanating from the playroom. Frantically rushing out of the bathroom (every mom knows what this is like!), she found her eldest son, Wesley (then four), seated atop his little brother, pounding away. As she forcefully yanked Wesley off his brother, she pled with him, "Wesley, you must love your brother!"

"But he makes me so mad! I can't love him!" Wesley replied through angry tears.

As parents, we all can easily imagine a situation like this one. Now, if you were Wesley's dad or mom, how would you have answered him? Or, to put a finer point on it, how do you think a *Christian* parent should respond to a child who is angry, disobedient, and hopeless? And should a Christian's response differ significantly from what we might hear from a loving Mormon mom or a conscientious Jewish father? Of course, every parent would undoubtedly have restrained their son and told him that beating up his little brother was inappropriate behavior. But then what? What would come next? Is there something that would make a Christian's response distinctly Christian?

When raising our daughter, Jessica (along with her brothers James and Joel), I (Elyse) would have answered a cry of "I can't love my brother!" in this way: "Oh, yes, you can, and you will! God says that you must love your brother and you'd better start . . . or else!" Would your answer have been different from mine? In what way? And how would you know if your reply was a distinctly Christian one? After all, it's obvious that just because we're Christian parents, it doesn't necessarily follow that our parenting is essentially Christian. Frequently, it's something else entirely.

Where Did Those Easy Steps Go?

Because parenting is one of those learn-as-you-go endeavors, books and seminars about doing it well are in high demand. And because most parents are stretched for time, we especially appreciate teachers and writers who give us a tidy list of three foolproof steps we can memorize in an afternoon while the kids enjoy a playdate with their friends.

Learning how to answer questions like the one posed above is probably one of the primary reasons you've picked up this book. You're wondering what to say when it seems like your kids just aren't getting it and seem to be going in the wrong direction. How should a Christian parent respond to the disobedience, selfishness, hopelessness, or sullenness that so frequently mark the lives of our children? Conversely, how should we respond when they seem to be outwardly compliant but are obviously not changed from within?

Jessica and I understand. We know you need answers. You want to be a faithful parent, or you wouldn't be bothering with this book. Like you, we long to be faithful parents too. But both of us are not only parents who want to be faithful; we're also people who have been transformed by the message of the gospel of grace. So, yes, this book will help you when you ask, "How am I supposed to respond to *that* kind of behavior?" But that's not its primary purpose.

This book will provide you with something more than a three-step formula for successful parenting. Even though it might seem counterintuitive, none of us need more rules or law. In this case, law might masquerade as "easy steps," "hints for success," or even "secret formulas," but make no mistake, at heart they are all law. Moralistic people share the hope that rules can improve and transform us, but Christians don't. Christians know that rules can't save us—what we need is a Savior. History has proven that no one responds well to rules (Rom. 3:23). You and I see this in our lives as well. Just think back to your latest New Year's resolution. How's that going for you? Yeah, me too. God has given us a perfect law (7:12), but none of us—no, not one—have obeyed it perfectly or with our whole heart (3:10). So, why would we think that our success rate to raise our children well would be any greater if we just had different rules or more steps?

In light of our dismal record, it should be obvious that the foundation of our parenting must come from somewhere or someone else. This source has to give us something we don't have—something more than rules to obey. But what else is there? There is grace, and this grace is found in Jesus. Grace is what Jessica and I want to give to you, too, so you can give it to your children in turn. Our salvation (and our kids') is by grace alone through faith alone in Christ alone. Parenting too, then, is by grace alone.

Most of us are painfully aware we're not perfect parents. We're also deeply grieved that our kids bear the wounds of our imperfections and experience that imperfection in themselves. But the remedy to our mutual imperfections isn't more rules, even if it seems like it might produce outwardly tidy or polite children. Christian children (and their parents) don't need to learn to be "nice." They need the death and resurrection of a Savior who has gone before them as a faithful high priest who was a child himself, who lived and died perfectly in their place, and who extends the offer of complete forgiveness, total righteousness, and indissoluble adoption to all who will believe. This is the message we all need.

We need the gospel of grace and the grace of the gospel. Our children can't use God's law any more than we can because they will respond to it the same way we do. They'll ignore it or bend it or obey it outwardly for selfish purposes, but this one thing is certain: they won't obey it from the heart because they can't. That's why Jesus had to die.

I understand that right about now you might be getting a little uncomfortable with what I'm saying. You might be wondering what I mean by "God's rule" or "the law," and why I'm saying that our kids don't need it. Don't be discouraged. We'll work through the whys and hows of raising children in Christ alone, though it might look very different from the way you're doing it right now.

Have They Heard the Message?

Christians know the gospel is a message unbelievers need to hear. We tell them they can't earn their way into heaven and they have to trust in Jesus alone for their goodness. But then something odd happens when we start training the miniature unbelievers in our own homes. We forget everything we know about the deadliness of relying on our own goodness and teach them that Christianity is all about their behavior and whether on any given day God is pleased or displeased with them. It's no wonder that so many children from Christian homes are lost as they seek meaning in life, basing their identity in anything other than God and rejecting the faith they were raised in.

There is no easy way to say it, but it must be said: parents and churches are not passing on a robust Christian faith and an accompanying commitment to the church. We can take some solace in the fact that many children do eventually return. But Christian parents and churches need to ask the hard question, What is it about our faith commitment that does not find root in the lives of our children?

The primary reason I believe the majority of kids from Christian homes stray from the faith is because they never really heard the gospel or had it to begin with. They were taught that God wants them to be good, that poor Jesus is sad when they disobey, and that asking Jesus into their hearts is the full breadth and depth of the gospel message. Scratch the surface of the faith of the young people around you, and you'll find a disturbing deficiency in understanding the most basic tenets of Christianity. This is illustrated by a conversation I recently had with a young woman in her early twenties who had been raised in a Christian home and who had attended church for most of her life.

After she had assured me that she was, indeed, saved, I asked her, "What does it mean to be a Christian?"

"It means you ask Jesus into your heart."

"Yes, all right, but what does that mean?"

"It means you ask Jesus to forgive you."

"Okay, but what do you ask him to forgive you for?"

"Bad things? I guess you ask him to forgive you for bad things, um, the sins you do."

"Like what?"

A deer in the headlights stared back at me. I thought I'd try a different tack.

"Why would Jesus forgive you?"

She fidgeted. "Um, because you ask him?"

Okay, I thought, *I'll try again.*

"What do you think God wants you to know?"

She beamed. "He wants me to know that I should love myself and that there's nothing I can't do if I think I can."

"And what does God want from you?" I asked.

"He wants me to do good stuff."

"Like?"

The deer reappeared.

"You know, be nice to others and don't hang around with bad people," she said at last.

Be Good for Goodness' Sake

Of course, you might say that this superficiality is an aberration and not typical of the kids in your home or church. I hope you're right. Or maybe you aren't even sure how to answer those questions yourself. We all have to admit that if a majority of our children are leaving the faith as soon as they can, and if we're not even sure how to express our faith, something has gone terribly wrong. Certainly, the faith that has empowered the persecuted church for two millennia isn't as thin and boring as "Say you're sorry," "Be nice," and "Don't be like *them*." Why would anyone want to deny themselves, lay down their lives, or suffer for something as inane as that? Aside from the "Ask Jesus into your heart" part, how does this message differ from what any unchurched child hears every day?

Let's face it: most of our children believe God is happy if they're "good for goodness' sake." We've transformed the holy, awesome, magnificent, and loving God of the Bible into Santa and his elves. And instead of transmitting the gloriously liberating and life-changing truths of the gospel, we've taught our children that what God wants from them is primarily their happiness, politeness, and a shallow form of morality. We've told them being good and feeling good (at least outwardly) are the be-all and end-all of their faith. This isn't the gospel; we're not handing down Christianity. We need less of *Daniel Tiger* and *Adventures in Odyssey* and tons more of the radical, bloody, scandalous message of God made man for us to free us from our sin.

This other thing we're giving them has a name. It's called *moralism*. Here's how one seminary professor described his childhood experience in church:

> The preachers I regularly heard in the . . . church in which I was raised tended to interpret and preach Scripture without Christ as the central . . . focus. Characters like Abraham and Paul were commended as models of sincere faith and loyal obedience. . . .

On the other hand, men like Adam and Judas were criticized as the antithesis of proper moral behavior. Thus Scripture became nothing more than a source book for moral lessons on Christian living whether good or bad.[1]

When we change the story of the Bible from the gospel of grace to a book of moralistic teachings like Aesop's fables, all sorts of things go wrong. Unbelieving children are encouraged to display the fruit of the Holy Spirit even though they are spiritually dead in their trespasses and sins (Eph. 2:1). Unrepentant children are taught to say they're sorry and ask for forgiveness even though they've never tasted true godly sorrow. They are told they are pleasing to God because they've achieved some "moral victory." Good manners have been elevated to the level of Christian righteousness. Some parents discipline their kids until they evince a prescribed form of contrition, and others work hard at keeping their children away from the wickedness in the world, assuming the brokenness within their children has been handled because they prayed a prayer one time at Bible club, youth camp, or VBS. Instead of the gospel of grace, we've given them daily baths in a "sea of narcissistic moralism,"[2] and they respond to such rules and moralism the same way we do—they run for the closest exit as soon as they can.

Moralistic parenting occurs because most of us have a wrong view of the Bible. The story of the Bible isn't a story about making good little boys and girls better. As Sally Lloyd-Jones writes in *The Jesus Storybook Bible*,

> Now, some people think the Bible is a book of rules, telling you what you should and shouldn't do. The Bible certainly does have some rules in it. They show you how life works best. But the Bible isn't mainly about you and what you should be doing. It's about God and what he has done. Other people think the Bible is a book of heroes, showing you people you should copy. The Bible does have some heroes in it, but . . . most of the people

in the Bible aren't heroes at all. They make some big mistakes (sometimes on purpose), they get afraid and run away. At times they are downright mean. *No, the Bible isn't a book of rules, or a book of heroes.* The Bible is most of all a Story. It's an adventure story about a young Hero who comes from a far country to win back his lost treasure. It's a love story about a brave Prince who leaves his palace, his throne—everything—to rescue the one he loves. It's like the most wonderful of fairy tales that has come true in real life.[3]

This is the story our children need to hear, and, like us, they need to hear it over and over again.

You're a Christian Parent, but Is Your Parenting Christian?

Grace, or the free favor that has been lavished on us through Christ, ought to make our parenting radically different from what unbelievers do. That's because the good news of God's grace is meant to permeate and transform every relationship we have, including our relationships with our children. All the typical ways we construct to get things done and get others to do our bidding are simply obliterated by a gospel message that tells us we are all both *radically sinful* and *radically loved*. At the deepest level of what we do as parents, we should hear the heartbeat of a loving, grace-giving Father who freely adopts rebels and transforms them into loving sons and daughters. If this is not the message your children hear from you, if the message you send them on a daily basis is about being good so that you won't be disappointed, then the gospel needs to transform your parenting too.

And now, back to the little vignette we opened our introduction with. You'll remember we left Wesley after he had just cried out, "I can't love my brother!" The Christian response to his cry isn't what I would have said: "Oh, yes, you can and you will. The Bible says you have to, so you can."

No, the Christian response to a statement like, "I can't love my brother!" is something more along these lines:

> Exactly! I am so glad to hear you say that because it shows me God is working in you. It is true that God commands you to love your brother, Wesley, but you can't. That is the bad news, but that is not all the news there is. The rest of the news is so exciting! You can't love your brother like God is asking you to, so you need a Rescuer to help you. And the really great news is that God has already sent one! His name is Jesus. Jesus has perfectly loved you and has perfectly loved your brother for you. If you believe in him, he doesn't punish you the way you were punishing and beating up your brother. Instead, he's taken all the punishment you deserve when he died on the cross for you. He knows how angry you are. He knows there are times you're mean and selfish. But he loves you despite your sin. And because of this, Wesley, because of the way you've been lavishly loved, if you believe in him, you will grow to love your brother more and more. But you'll never be able to do this consistently and wholeheartedly without a changed heart.

Jessica did respond to Wesley with soul-comforting words like these, then continued with a time of correction and prayer for him that God would grant him faith to believe the Rescuer he needed loved him, would forgive him, and would help him love others too.

He's the Faithful Father

It's true that Jessica and I don't always respond with grace like this, nor do our children always listen when we do. Sometimes they roll their eyes; other times they pretend to listen but don't hear a word we say. Sometimes we're sure they're thinking, *Grace, gospel, blah, blah, blah.* Frequently, what might have been a wonderful grace moment becomes nothing more than correction and prayer for grace. Sometimes we're distracted or in a hurry or discouraged or apathetic, and we don't have the time or the inclination to give grace to our children. Sometimes we ignore them and wish we could have an afternoon alone. We're just like you.

Although we long to be faithful parents, we also rest in the truth that our faithfulness is not what will save our children. Giving grace to our children is not another formula that guarantees their salvation or obedience. Grace parenting is not another law for you to master to perfect your parenting or your children. Your children will be saved *only* through the faithfulness of the Holy Spirit who works at the direction of our heavenly Father. He's the powerful, soul-transforming One. Yes, he may use parents as means to accomplish his purpose, but salvation is *entirely* of the Lord (Jonah 2:9).

If the gospel message we've been presenting in this introduction is something new or foreign to you, turn to the appendix at the back of this book to learn more. Wouldn't it be wonderful to know the kind of love we've been talking about and be able to rest in God's faithfulness to empower you to parent your children well?

Remember God's Grace

As we begin our journey together, first and foremost Jessica and I want you to remember: it's all about God's grace. It is our prayer that the grace we've been given will bud and flower into a harvest of grace-filled, joyous children who delight in God's great love for them in Christ.

She and I have collaborated on this project for years, and her "feet on the ground" perspective is what has made this book something more than the musings of a grandmother sitting in a quiet and tidy house writing prose. That said, when "I" appears, it's Elyse talking (unless otherwise indicated). At the end of every chapter are questions that will challenge your thinking and help you clarify important principles. Please take the time to work through them.

PART 1

Foundations of Grace

1

From Teaching Rules to Giving Grace

I found that the very commandment that was intended to bring life actually brought death.

Romans 7:10

A mom and her three children were all seated on the floor in the brightly colored playroom. It was time for their Bible game. Joshua and Caleb loved the game because they usually got all the answers right, but Jordan, the middle child, was alternately sullen and disruptive.

"Who wants to draw the first card?" Mom asked.

Two hands shot up simultaneously. "I do, I do!" Joshua and Caleb chimed.

"Okay, Joshua, you go first."

Joshua picked a card from the pile and read, "Tell the story of Jonah in your own words, and then talk about what the story means to you."

Joshua then proceeded to talk about Jonah being commanded to serve God but he was disobedient, so instead he got swallowed by a whale. Afterward the whale vomited him up onto the ground (the three boys giggled), and then Jonah obeyed God.

"Good job, Joshua! Now, what does the story teach us?" Mom asked.

Caleb's hand was the first one up. "It means we should obey when God tells us to do something like go tell people about God."

"Right, Caleb! Now, can you think of some ways to tell people about God?"

Different answers were shouted out. "We could bake cookies for our neighbors and invite them to church!" "We could offer to do chores for them too!"

"Yes," Mom said. "That's exactly right. Now, Jordan, can you tell me what you could do to obey God?"

Jordan stammered out a weak "I don't know."

"Can't you think of anything at all?"

Becoming more defiant, Jordan shouted, "No, and I don't want to!"

"But, Jordan, you don't want to get swallowed by a whale, do you? God tells us to serve our neighbors and tell them about him. If you can't be good, you won't get any Goldfish crackers or the blue Jello I've made."

Sadly, many Christian parents can relate to this painful little story. In an effort to teach our children about the Bible, we frequently employ the stories in the Bible as a way to compel obedience. Can you picture doing something like that with your kids? I know I can. In fact, that's exactly the way I used the Bible when I was raising my children. I can remember a little song we sang that went something like, "I don't want to be a Jonah and get swallowed by a whale. So to Nineveh I will go, for the Lord has told me so, and I'll shout aloud, 'You must be born again!'"

I took every story in the Bible and made it about what my children were supposed to be doing. I took every story of grace and mercy (like Jonah's) and made it one of law and morals ("You'd better obey. There are whales about!"). Just like the seminary professor's pastor we learned about in the introduction, I didn't give my kids the gospel story. I assumed they had heard it enough times and therefore believed it. Jesus and the cross? That was old news. The real action was in obeying, not in remembering. What I didn't know then was that the good news of Jesus's obedience and death was the only motif that would grant my children a heart to obey. So we ate Goldfish and blue Jello, sang songs about Jonah, and worried about whales.

Right about now you might be wondering if I'm saying that parents should never give their children any rules. I'm not saying that at all. Every parent *must* give their children guidance, direction, and rules. What I am saying is that these things are not to be the primary theme of our teaching. Jesus Christ and the work he's *already* done are.

Over the next several pages, you'll read about the different kinds of rules parents are to give their children along with the kinds of obedience that these rules may produce. But for now, take a moment and ask yourself what percentage of your time is spent in *declaring the rules* and what percentage is spent in *reciting the gospel story*. Of course, if your children are very young, it is certainly understandable if most of your time is spent with the rules. You can't have long discussions about theology with a two-year-old. Even so, you can begin to bring the good news about Jesus's work as soon as they are able to understand.

Now that you've thought about whether you give your children more rules or gospel, you can recite the story of the Rescuer to yourself:

Your Father so loved you that he sent his Son to rescue you from the penalty that was due you for your sins. These are the sins you committed when you were a child, the sins you committed before you became a believer, and the ones you've committed today. He has seen all of it—your selfishness, anger, laziness, and pride—*and* he has loved you. To rescue you, his Son was sent from heaven, his home, to be born as a human baby, live a perfect life, suffer in shame and humiliation and die on Calvary, rise again on the third day, and then ascend to the right hand of his Father, where he watches over and redeems every facet of your life, including your parenting. He has promised to work everything in your life for your transformation and the flourishing of your community. This is the kind of watchful, fatherly love he has for you. He is the perfect parent, and this record of perfection has been transferred to you, if you put your trust in him. He's a wonderful Father, and you can rest in his everlasting arms.

One of the reasons we don't share this story with our children is because it doesn't resonate deeply in our own hearts. As one mom of four told Jessica and me, "I couldn't teach my kids about the gospel before because it was not real to me and had no impact on me. Although I was a Christian, I was trying to save myself by following the rules and expecting my kids to be saved in the same way 'or else. . . .' Praise God that although I mess up every day with them, I am learning to direct them to their need for him and not their need to do good or to please me."

Our Obedience and the Rules

The following discussion about rules and obedience is obviously not everything parents should say to their kids. It is simply an introduction to different forms of moralistic rules and obedience and a way to differentiate them from true Christian righteousness.[1]

Initial Obedience

Every responsible parent knows there are certain things their children must be taught. The littlest kids need to know, understand, and respond immediately to the command "No," which is why it is usually one of the first words they learn to say. They need to be taught "Stop," and "Come to me," for the same reasons. These words are so obviously important they hardly need mentioning. When a child begins to dash out into a busy street, their life may depend on whether they respond to your voice or not. Because every responsible parent, Christian or non-Christian, teaches these concepts to their children, they don't have anything to do with a right standing before God, but that doesn't mean they're not important. These are simply concepts that will protect children from harm and begin to enable them to function within their family and society.

Social Obedience

As little ones mature, they are taught to say "Please" and "Thank you" and begin learning the social mores of their particular culture. For instance, in some cultures, burping loudly after a meal is a sign of gratitude for good food, while in American culture it is usually considered boorish. These rules or laws about polite behavior are transient from one era to another and from one country (or region) to another. Manners in America's Deep South differ significantly from those in the Northeast and the Southwest, for example. Because the Bible doesn't instruct us in etiquette, good manners are not a matter of Christian righteousness, although that doesn't mean we shouldn't teach them to our children.

Of course, if a child has been told not to burp at the dinner table but deliberately continues to do so, this disobedience is more than just a manners issue. It may be an issue of defiance, which then transfers the behavior into a higher category. It may be sinful if they are being willfully disobedient.

We will talk more about this later, but for now remember that the social conventions of any particular culture don't have anything to do with one's standing before a holy God. Even if little Johnny never burped at the table, it doesn't mean he has right standing before God. It may simply mean he has good digestion, he can't burp on demand, or he is a pleaser by nature and doesn't want to make anyone mad at him. The kingdom of God is not a matter of burping or slurping. It is about righteousness, peace, and joy in the Holy Spirit (Rom. 14:12).

Civic Obedience

Children must also be taught to be law-abiding citizens. That means they are instructed in the laws of the land in which they live and are told they must obey them. This is another category of law that every responsible parent teaches their children. All children, Christian or not, must be taught not to cheat on tests or steal. They must learn that lying has consequences and that disobeying those in legitimate authority, whether parents, teachers, or police, is unacceptable unless injustice or wrong is being done by them.

Jessica's son Wesley needed to learn that he could not beat up anyone who got in his way. This, too, is not a matter of Christian righteousness. It is simply a matter of learning how to get along with other people in a world where they might have the propensity to get in your way or mess with your Nintendo Switch. While it is true that you should not haul off and punch any person who displeases you, it's also true that an unbelieving pacificist and an unbelieving bully are both separated from God's love. Of course, it's better for a family and society to be peace-loving rather than violent and abusive, but ultimately before God, only Christ's righteousness will suffice.

Religious Obedience

Religious obedience is what we teach children to do as part of a life of faith before they come to faith. For instance, we ask them to wait before we eat so we can thank God for our food. This is usually nothing more than a religious exercise for them. They learn when to stand up in church, when to sing, and when to sit quietly. They learn to give their pennies in Sunday school.

We call this *religious* obedience because it has to do with the practices of the faith but is not necessarily the fruit of saving faith.

It may be the fruit of any number of things, including a desire to avoid correction or a desire to feel good about their own obedience. Of course, it may also be the fruit of real faith, but we must never assume that because children close their eyes when the family prays, they're saved. Outward conformity to religious exercises is not proof of saving faith.

Training children in religious obedience is not wrong. We are commanded to do so. We are told to teach them the Bible, to talk with them about God's nature and works, to pray in their presence, and to take them to worship (Exod. 12:26–28; Deut. 4:9–10; 6:7–9; Ps. 78:4–8; Eph. 6:4). But telling children they are good or that God is pleased with them because they closed their eyes during prayer time is both dangerous and false.

So, what should a parent say to encourage little four-year-old Benjamin who always fidgets and causes distractions when he is finally able to sit quietly for five minutes while the family prays? You might say something like this:

> Bennie, I'm thankful the Lord helped you to sit quietly tonight. I know that's hard for you because you've got so many wiggles and you don't understand what we're doing. But on nights like tonight, when you are able to sit quietly, it's because God is helping you learn to obey. Someday you'll know how wonderful he is and how much he loves you whether you wiggle or not. Then you'll want to talk with him too. But for tonight I just want you to know that your quiet sitting helps me know that he's working in your heart. Now, where did those wiggles get to?

On the other hand, you might be wondering what you should say when Bennie disrupts, wiggles, and talks during the prayer time. You might say,

> Do you know why we love to pray, Bennie? We love to pray because our hearts were just like yours. We never wanted to spend five minutes of our time talking to God; all we wanted to do was have fun,

and it didn't seem like fun to talk to God. But then God changed our hearts so we could see how amazing he is. He showed us that even though we didn't love him or like to talk to him, he loved us anyway. And when you find out how kind someone has been to you, and how amazing their love is for you, it makes you want to talk to them. Honestly, there are still times I don't want to sit and talk to God, but even in those times he loves me just the same as the times when I love talking to him.

But do you know what is more important than sitting still during prayer? Having a God who loves you no matter what is more important. Understanding how your heart would be hard and disobedient all the time without his help is more important. And asking Jesus to change your heart to love him and to forgive you for not loving him is the most important thing of all. Now, Bennie, we have talked to you previously about disrupting family prayer. I understand your heart is not drawn to God during prayer yet. I am glad you are not pretending to pray with us, because that would be lying. I am praying God changes your heart so you will want to pray with us. But until that happens, you need to sit quietly during prayer time. Your behavior is a distraction to those of us who want to pray, so I am reminding you this behavior will result in correction.

There is a marked difference between this kind of gracious parenting and the moralistic parenting I did when I was raising my children. I would alternately tell them they were "good" when they sat quietly or tell them they had to close their eyes and pray or they would be disciplined because they were being "bad." My parenting had very little to do with the gospel. I assumed my children had regenerate hearts because they'd prayed a prayer at some point, and I required religious obedience from them. This resulted in kids who were alternately hypocritical and rebellious. It taught them how to feign prayer without pressing them to long for the Savior who loves hypocrites and rebels.

Religious obedience is probably the most difficult and danger-ous form of obedience simply because it is so easily confused with conformity to God's plan. It's the place where most Christian families go terribly wrong. Yes, we are commanded to teach our children to read God's Word, pray, and worship. But their acquiescence to these things won't save them. Only the righteous life, death, and resurrection of Jesus Christ can save them.

By way of reminder, then, we have demonstrated four levels of rules and corresponding obedience: basic instruction in hearing and obeying, social rules or manners, civic rules and submission to human authority, and, finally, religious training. None of these levels of obedience earn God's favor. None of them can earn approval from God. In fact, each of these forms of obedience may actually keep a compliant child ignorant of their need for a Savior. But that's where the law of God comes in.

God's Beautiful, Holy, Good . . . and Crushing Law

The apostle Paul, a Jewish rabbi who had extensive respect for and acquaintance with God's law (Acts 22:3), had some very shocking thoughts about it once he came to faith in Christ. Although he heartily agreed it was "holy, righteous and good" (Rom. 7:12), and although he knew the beautiful nature of God's law, he also knew the law could never bring sinners to life because *no one* could obey it. He confessed that all of his obedience (and it was extensive) had no more value than a pile of manure (Phil. 3:8). He wrote:

> No one will be declared righteous in God's sight by the works of the law. (Rom. 3:20)

> What shall we conclude then? Do we have any advantage? Not at all! For we have already made the charge that Jews and Gentiles alike are all under the power of sin. As it is written: "There is no one righteous, not even one; there is no one who understands; there is no one who seeks God." (vv. 9–11)

All [Jews and Gentiles] have sinned and fall short of the glory of God. (v. 23)

I found that the very commandment [to obey the law (Deut. 30:16)] that was intended to bring life actually brought death [because although I tried, I couldn't obey it]. (7:10)

For all who rely on works of the law are under a curse; for it is written, "Cursed be everyone who does not abide by all things written in the Book of the Law, and do them." Now it is evident that no one is justified before God by the law [because our ongoing failure to obey keeps us from God's blessing]. (Gal. 3:10–11 ESV)

[The law is a] ministry that brought death, which was engraved in letters on stone. (2 Cor. 3:7)

You who are trying to be justified by the law have been alienated from Christ; you have fallen away from grace. (Gal. 5:4)

These words about God's law and our condition of lawlessness should make us stop and seriously question how we use it in our own lives and in the lives of our children. When we seek to have right standing (justification) before a holy God through compliance to the law, we are *severed, cut off, separated,* and *alienated* from the grace and righteousness provided by Jesus Christ. We're on our own. When we teach our children to do the same thing, we are training them in a "ministry that brought death." Why death? Because that's the inevitable result when people ignore Jesus Christ and seek the good life on their own.

This is serious business. It is no wonder, then, that the great reformer Martin Luther wrote, "The law of God, the most salutary [beneficial] doctrine of life, cannot advance humans on their way to righteousness, but rather hinders them."[2] The law of God, although beneficial and beautiful, cannot advance us on our way to righteousness because we *cannot obey it.* Although the law demands perfection in only two areas, none of us (reread the passages above if you need to)—no, *none of us*—fully complies. What are these two areas? Jesus laid them out for us in Matthew 22:35–40.

> One of them, an expert in the law, tested him with this question: "Teacher, which is the great commandment in the Law?"
>
> Jesus replied: "'Love the Lord your God with all your heart and with all your soul and with all your mind.' This is the first and greatest commandment. And the second is like it: 'Love your neighbor as yourself.' All the Law and the Prophets hang on these two commandments."

Pure, unadulterated, consistent love for God and pure, unadulterated, consistent love for others is the summation of all the law God has given us in the Bible. Of course, the problem is that we never wholeheartedly or consistently obey these simple commands. We love ourselves more than we love God or others. We're always erecting false gods in our own hearts and worshiping and serving them. We're always more focused on what we want and how we might get it than we are on loving God and laying down our lives for others. The law does show us the right way to live, but none of us obeys it perfectly. Not for one millisecond.

Even though our believing children do not consistently obey God's law, we do need to teach it to them again and again. And when they tell us they can't love God or others, we don't argue with them. We agree with them and tell them of their need for a Savior.

The law of God also hinders our advance toward righteousness because we think that if we just try hard enough or are sorry enough, we'll be able to obey it. We read the promises of life for obedience, God's instruction to "carefully follow the terms of this covenant, so that you may prosper in everything you do" (Deut. 29:9), and think that means we can do it. The promises of life for obedience are not meant to build our self-confidence. They're meant to make us long for obedience, and then, when we fail *again*, compel us to let go of our own goodness and drive us to Christ.

In addition, the law defeats us by awakening the sin resident within us. As Paul said,

> I would not have known what sin was had it not been for the law. For I would not have known what coveting really was if the law had not said, "You shall not covet." But sin, seizing the opportunity afforded by the commandment, produced in me every kind of coveting. For apart from the law, sin was dead. (Rom. 7:7–8)

In other words, the very law meant to bring life stirs up a desire to rebel against it and, therefore, sin. Again, that doesn't mean we don't teach our children God's law. We're commanded to do so, in order that they can see their need for a Savior. The law won't make them good, but it will make them turn from the hope of ever being good enough and open them to the love, sacrifice, and welcome of their Savior, Jesus Christ. Yes, teach your children God's law and how he commands obedience. But before you're done, give them grace and explain again the beautiful story of Christ's perfect keeping of the law for them and how his righteousness is imparted to us when we trust in him. This is the message we all need to hear, and it is the only message that will transform our hearts.

The Gospel or Law

Everything that isn't gospel is law. I'll say it again: *everything that isn't gospel is law.* Every way we try to make our kids good that isn't rooted in the good news of the life, death, resurrection, and ascension of Jesus Christ is damnable, crushing, despair-breeding, Pharisee-producing law. We won't get the results we want from the law. We'll either get shallow self-righteousness or blazing rebellion or both (and frequently from the same kid on the same day). We'll get moralistic kids who are cold and hypocritical and look down on others or kids who are rebellious and self-indulgent and can't wait to get out of the house. We have to remember that, in the life of our unbelieving children, the law is given for one reason only: to turn them from trying to save themselves and lead them to Christ.

You remember that little game with the mom and her three sons at the beginning of the chapter, right? How would that game have been different if that mom remembered that every Bible story is about God's grace through Jesus Christ and the gospel? After Joshua recited the bare facts of Jonah's story, his mother would have drawn out its real meaning. The story of Jonah isn't about learning to be obedient or facing the consequences. It's about how God is merciful to both religiously self-righteous, unloving Jonah and the irreligious, violent unbelievers of Nineveh. It's about God's ability to save souls and how he invites us to partner with him to be conduits of his grace even when we disobey. It's about God's mercy, not our obedience.

Here's how the conversation would differ if that mom gave gospel instead of law.

"Good job, Joshua! Now what does the story teach us?" Mom asked.

Caleb's hand was the first one up. "It means we should obey when God tells us to do something like go tell people about God."

"Yes, Caleb, we are to obey God, but that's not the primary message of the story. Can you think of any other message?"

Jordan piped up. "Lots of times people don't want to obey God."

"Right, Jordan! That's exactly right. I know it's hard for me to obey. I'm just like Jonah too. This story is a message about how kind and merciful God is. He was kind to the bad people from Nineveh because he didn't destroy them even though they deserved it. He was kind to them by helping them believe the message Jonah told them. But he was also kind to Jonah. Even though Jonah didn't love his neighbors (the people from Nineveh), God didn't leave him to die in the belly of the big fish, although that was what Jonah deserved. Instead, God gave him another chance and kept giving him chances even though Jonah didn't really love God's merciful nature.

"God gives us so many opportunities to obey him because he loves us and is so merciful. God shows us how he loves us. His dear Son, Jesus, spent three days in a very dark place just like Jonah did. Jesus spent three days in a grave after dying for our sins. But then he rose again from the dead so that we could be good in God's eyes and tell other people about how loving he is. Can you think of some things we could do so that other people would know about God's love?"

Different answers were shouted out. "We could bake cookies for our neighbors and invite them to church!" "We could offer to do chores for them too!"

"Right! Now, let's celebrate God's mercy and have a party with some Goldfish crackers and blue Jello I've made."

Remembering God's Grace

Pay attention to what the Holy Spirit might be doing in your heart through this chapter. Take the time to think deeply about it and answer the following questions.

1) In what ways do you use the Bible as a rule book instead of as the good news?

2) How can remembering and retelling the gospel change the way you parent?

3) How does the good news of Jesus help your kids when they fail to obey?

_____

_____

2

How the Gospel Makes Our Kids Good

So we are made right with God through faith and not by obeying the law.

Romans 3:28 NLT

Into the nothingness and vacuity of the formless void, God, the Creative Love, spoke, "Let there be light!" and light burst forth. Iridescent colors danced into the universe. Shimmering prisms of living light suffused splendor into the air. The Father, Son, and Spirit rejoiced in what they saw. The Creative Love smiled. He declared, "You're good!"[1]

Day after day, the depth and complexity of his work multiplied as God filled emptiness with glory. Light and darkness, heaven and earth, seas and land, plants and trees and stars and moons—all beloved, all beautiful, all good! Fish and birds swarmed and flocked. Eagles and parrots, great sea creatures, and tiny krill entered into God's joy in himself and his creation. It was a thundering, harmonious hymn in celebration of life, wisdom, power, and goodness. Livestock and creeping things and beasts of the earth sprang into being at the sound of his voice. "You are good! Live! Be fruitful! Multiply! Rejoice!" In pure bliss, they dashed to do his bidding, each singing with their unique voice.

Then, finally, on the sixth day, all was ready. God's beautiful new home was decorated and replete with an excess of splendor and provision. The grand celebration was about to begin, and it was time for the honored guests to arrive. He took into his hand some of the ground he had made. He fashioned it with care and breathed into it his breath of life.

He spoke to it, "Image me! You are my mirror. You, above all else that I have made, will display my goodness."

Adam and Eve breathed in, and the first thing they saw was the living Word. He smiled at his children. "I have created you to be like me, and so you are. You will love and desire goodness because I am good and have made you good. This earth is yours. Guard it, tend it, fill it with millions. Now sing with me and rejoice, for I have made you to know me and to love me and to be known and loved by me. You are blessed above all that I have created."

Then God looked over the feast. Like a lordly host at a long-anticipated reception, he pondered all he had made. He declared: "You are very good!" At his word, choirs in the heavens and on the earth filled his feast with majestic melody, harmony, and rhythm. The morning stars sang, the trees of the fields clapped their hands, the mountains bowed low in worship. "The Lord is good, and he has made us good! Hurray for our loving God! Hurray for his good creation!"

The End of Our Goodness Until Goodness Came

Then, in one fell swoop, the lie was believed, the goodness was doubted, and all was lost. Rather than celebrating the goodness it had been given, all there was became "subjected to futility [and] bondage to corruption," and relentless, painful groaning (Rom. 8:20–22 ESV). Misery, suspicion, sickness, wandering, and destitution of heart replaced the majestic music and celebration. Death filled God's beautiful home so that it was no longer wholly good. The goodness of all he made had been wrecked. In place of the Lord's benediction and approval, wrath and the curse would reign.

Banished from their home, Adam and Eve, like shattered mirrors, became strangers isolated from one another and from God. The desperate search to regain goodness began. Their anguished, futile efforts at goodness supplanted the joyful benediction of "You are good!" And so, in desperation to hear it once again, they sought ways to earn it for themselves. In furious envy, their firstborn son murdered his younger brother because he did not attain it while his brother did. *Is Abel's offering good and mine bad, God? Fine, I'll just kill him, since you think he's so great!* (This isn't merely ancient history. The apostle John warns us, "Do not be like Cain, who belonged to the evil one and murdered his brother. And why did he murder him? *Because his own actions were evil and his brother's were righteous*" [1 John 3:12].) Cain idolized God's approval for his own work, and in furious envy he chose murder. His descendants would create pejorative names for those who loved to feel good about how hard they worked: "holier-than-thou," "self-righteous prig," "goodie-two-shoes." They would emulate them or murder them in their hearts (Matt. 5:21–22) to silence the voice of self-condemnation.

Later in Genesis, in an effort to prove they no longer needed God's help to restore their goodness, the people of Babel rose up to build a tower to their own honor and bestow the benediction upon themselves. "Wow! Look at that!" they said. "We're great! We're good!" Rather than telling them that their efforts were a nice try, God scattered them by confusing their speech, and the people wandered apart (Gen. 11). This is our history, the legacy of every person who ever drew breath and tried to prove they really were good. Every person but One.

How did God respond to such wickedness? In righteous justice, he could have put an end to humanity. But he didn't. Instead, he sent the only one who was good—Jesus—back into his world. Jesus was born as a baby in Bethlehem, and when he became a man, he burst onto the Judean landscape. While he was reestablishing our righteousness in the Jordan River, the earth once again heard the blessed benediction.

> Jesus replied, "Let it be so now; it is proper for us to do this to fulfill all righteousness." . . . As soon as Jesus was baptized, he went up out of the water. At that moment heaven was opened, and he saw the Spirit of God descending like a dove and alighting on him. And a voice from heaven said, *"This is my Son, whom I love; with him I am well pleased."* (Matt. 3:15–17)

Jesus comes to fulfill all goodness and righteousness. Where we fail, he succeeds. He is circumcised for us, baptized for us. He responds to his parents' unjust questioning of his goodness with righteousness and truth (Luke 2:41–52). He loves his Father and his neighbor perfectly, and then he is stripped of all the reward of life and acceptance for the goodness he had earned. He is called a demon-possessed blasphemer. He is smitten for saying he was God. He doesn't hear "Good job!" but rather deafening silence. He receives the curse of God's abandonment. And, like Cain before us, we kill him in the name of goodness to rid our world of such audacity.

But Jesus doesn't sinfully crave God's approval; instead he worships God and loves us. He is goodness personified. Then, to vindicate him and prove that God's benediction rested upon him, God raises Jesus from the dead. In an outrageous demonstration of his love for his Son and his love for us, God transfers all of Jesus's goodness to us—if we would believe.

Praising Your Children Won't Make Them Good

So much of what we're advised to do as parents is to the end that our kids will "feel good" about themselves based on trying hard, being good at sports, bringing home good grades—in other words, their own efforts. This advice has roots in the modern self-esteem movement, which claimed that children's success in life is based on whether they feel like they are good or not. Although this self-esteem movement began in the 1950s–60s, this distortion of the truth is nothing new. It has been around for thousands of years. It's the same deception Adam and Eve believed in the beginning. *Yum*, they thought. *This fruit looks good, and it will make us good. Let's have it for dinner tonight.* Since then, we've been alternately telling ourselves that we're good, that if we try hard enough we'll be good enough, or that being good is an impossibility and we should just give up and have fun—after all, nobody's perfect!

In light of all this, what are parents to do? If we believe the Bible, we surely realize that neither parents nor children are truly good. But if, for example, all the other parents in the playgroup spend the day telling our kids how good they are for behaving well at the playground, how are we as Christian parents to respond?

Rather than merely telling our kids that they're good, we could say something like, "I noticed you shared your swing. Do you know what that reminds me of? How Christ shared his life with us. I'm so thankful for God working in your life that way. I know it's hard to be kind without God helping us, and you sharing shows that he's helping you!"

In case you're wondering whether the Bible gives an example of this kind of encouragement, here is Luke's report of what happened when Barnabas saw the grace of God working in the people of Antioch: "When he arrived and saw what the grace of God had done, he was glad and encouraged them all to remain true to the Lord with all their hearts" (Acts 11:23). Barnabas saw God's grace working in the lives of the people, so he exhorted them to remain faithful. We too can see God's grace at work in our children and exhort them to remain faithful.

Let's say that our children have a habit of selfishness, so before we drive them to their playdates, we spend some time praying together. We could simply thank God for sharing so much good, like friends, sunshine, and playdates, and then ask him to help them remember his generosity when others want what they are using. Then, if we notice them sharing, we could say something like this: "I'm so glad you're sharing! Isn't it great to see how God answered our prayer? You see, even though it's hard for us share, God is more powerful than our selfishness and can help us to share. Isn't he good?"

The one encouragement we can always give our children (and one another) is that God is more powerful than our sin and that he's strong and kind enough to help us want to do the right thing. We can assure them that his help can reach everyone, even them. Reminding them of God's goodness is how we teach our kids to grow up by grace alone.

We all long to be told, "You are good!" but only through the grace given to us in Jesus can we be made good and can our parenting be transformed to truly be by faith and grace alone. Praising our children won't make them good, but we can praise God for helping them, and in doing so, we show our children they're loved by God and show them how his love can transform them.

Human Obedience and Christian Righteousness

In the last chapter, we discussed four common levels of human rules and the resulting kinds of obedience we might expect from our children: initial, social, civic, and religious law and obedience. These four levels are what we are going to call "human obedience."

As you can see, what we're calling "human obedience" is the sort of obedience our children can do that is generally good for

Human Obedience

Initial Obedience	Learning to obey a parent's voice
Social Obedience	Learning social codes and manners
Civic Obedience	Learning to obey the laws of society
Religious Obedience	Learning the religious practices of family and church

the family and society. Human obedience encompasses the entire breadth of human goodness. This obedience or outward goodness is achievable by every person, saved or unsaved, because of God's common grace.[2] In some ways, society is certainly better off if people observe social, civic, and religious laws—if people try to be good to each other. It is more advantageous to live in a land of peace and freedom than strife and slavery (Titus 3:1–2). Respect, courtesy, and civil obedience are blessings from the Lord, who bestows his blessings on both the just and unjust (Matt. 5:45).

But if our human obedience isn't motivated by gratitude for God's grace, it is very dangerous. If not rooted in gratitude for God's love for us in Christ, morality is deadlier to the soul than immorality. Why? Remember Jesus said it was those who are lost, those who know they need a physician, whom he came to save (Luke 19:10). Those who excel at the kinds of obedience listed above may not see their need for a Savior; their hearts may be hardened and unfazed by God's grace. It was the woman who knew that she was forgiven for much who loved much (7:47). Forgiveness for deep offenses breeds deep love. Forgiveness for perceived and reasonable slights breeds apathetic disdain. A society riddled with immorality will not be a pleasant place to live. But a society riddled with self-congratulatory morality will be nice and tidy but resistant to grace and oh, so dead. And as we see in Scripture, such obedience might be only a breath away from murder, for it was the religious leaders, not the prostitutes, who called for the execution of the Christ.

Teaching our children to be well-behaved, good citizens is proper as far as it goes. But we must never mistake this training for Christian nurture or discipline, nor should we mistake acquiescence to social mores as true Christian righteousness. Christian righteousness is that level of goodness that can withstand the scrutiny of a perfectly holy God and earn the blessing, "You are good!" It is perfect obedience in both outward conformity and inward desire. It is goodness for the sake of God's great glory, motivated by a pure and zealous love for God and neighbor. It is the right action at the right time for the right reason. And a record of this kind of goodness can never be earned; it can only be bestowed by grace through faith.

Righteousness Bestowed

Christian righteousness differs from the kinds of obedience we're used to teaching our kids about. It is a goodness given by God to us out of his sheer generosity and mercy, and it rests squarely on the loving obedience and sacrifice of Jesus Christ alone. Christians have been teaching their children about this Christian righteousness for centuries. Some have taught their children about it by asking and answering key questions. Here's one of those question and answers about Christian righteousness from the Heidelberg Catechism:

> Q. How are you righteous before God?
>
> A. Only by true faith in Jesus Christ.
> Even though my conscience accuses me
> of having grievously sinned against all God's
>   commandments
> and of never having kept any of them,
> and even though I am still inclined toward all evil,
> nevertheless,
> without any merit of my own,
> out of sheer grace,

> God grants and credits to me
> the perfect satisfaction, righteousness, and holiness of
>   Christ,
> as if I had never sinned nor been a sinner,
> as if I had been as perfectly obedient
> as Christ was obedient for me.
> All I need to do
> is to accept this gift with a believing heart.[3]

Christian righteousness is different from human obedience because it is granted to us by God's grace, not because of our or our children's work. It is not something we can earn but rather it is a gift we are given even though we continue to fail terribly. The righteousness we are given is the very record of the righteousness of Jesus Christ. When a person has Christian righteousness, God looks upon that person as being perfectly obedient, no matter how they fail. God doesn't smile at us one day and then frown when we blow it the next day. When our children have been given the gift of Christian righteousness, God is always smiling at them because he sees them in his Son.

The way we receive this righteousness is by believing God is good and loving enough to give it to us and telling him that we want it more than we want our own self-generated goodness. The diagram below will help you understand the differences between human obedience and passive (what is done for us) righteousness.

Human Obedience vs. Passive Righteousness

Human Obedience	Passive Righteousness
Accessible to all who work	Accessible to all who believe
Outward conformity to rules and law	Record of Christ's obedience bestowed upon all who believe
Renewed by self-effort and resolutions	Initiated and renewed by the Holy Spirit
Temporary and fluctuating	Eternal and settled
Imperfect and incomplete	Perfect and complete

Grinding slavery of works	Grateful obedience of faith
Produces fear and insecurity	Produces peace and godly confidence
Results in pride and despair	Results in rest and joy

Sometimes this "Christian righteousness" is called justification. *Justification* is simply a word that means that our record is both "just as if we had never sinned" and also "just as if we had always obeyed." A justified person has a record of perfect obedience in God's eyes because the obedience of the perfect Son has been transferred to them by faith. Justified Christians are perfectly forgiven *and* perfectly righteous. When God looks at justified believers, parent or child, he sees us not only as forgiven (which is great news) but also as obedient and righteous (which is amazing). If Christian righteousness or justification is new to you, here are a few verses that demonstrate it:

For we maintain that a person is justified by faith *apart from the works of the law*. (Rom. 3:28)

[We] know that a person is *not justified by the works of the law, but by faith in Jesus Christ*. So we, too, have put our faith in Christ Jesus *that we may be justified by faith in Christ and not by the works of the law, because by the works of the law no one will be justified*. (Gal. 2:16)

Before the coming of this faith, we were held in custody under the law, locked up until the faith that was to come would be revealed. So the law was our guardian until Christ came that we might be *justified by faith*. (3:23–24)

In summary, then, this is what we have learned about our goodness or our righteousness bestowed: in the beginning, God declared that everything he had made was good. This benediction of goodness bestowed filled the hearts of all his creatures, and they rejoiced in him. Then sin entered, and our ability to attain true goodness was lost. Immediately people began to try to find goodness on their own. Eventually those who strove to be very good would kill the only truly good Man who ever lived. But even through this murderous act, God's perfect will was accomplished so that all who would believe would receive both forgiveness and righteousness.[4]

Better Than Charts and Stickers

Even though humanity's dismal lack of goodness (yes, even in our parenting!) has been repeating itself for thousands of years, we're still striving for our own goodness and training our children to do the same. We make charts for our children and give them stickers proclaiming, "You're great!" We plaster our cars with bumper stickers announcing that our kids are the best citizens in their class (even though every child in the class gets one). We tell them that making Mommy or Daddy happy by being good is the goal of life, thereby turning them into people who are enslaved to the opinions and approval of others and always hungering for more. And we instill within them the drive to prove themselves better than others, whether that's through being very, very good or very, very bad.

So, what can we offer our children that's better than stickers or charts? We can give them grace. We can offer joy and freedom. When they groan under the weight of what is required of them through the law and the rules of our parenting, we can give them this invitation:

> Taste and see that the Lord is good;
> blessed is the [kid] who takes refuge in him. (Ps. 34:8)

Keep displaying his goodness to your children. Do it over and over again. Point them to how good and loving God is, and then pray they will believe. They can only be made good by what Christ has done for them. Though there could be times when a reward system will need to be used, especially when children are young, make sure to incorporate grace into it.

The hope is that if, by God's grace, they believe and begin to transform, they will then obey out of gratitude and joy. They will see that grace frees them from the burden of not being able to be good on their own, and they will understand they can only be empowered to obey because of Jesus's perfect obedience to his Father.

Another reason we still want to give God's law to our children, even when they say they are saved, is to foster a heart of gratitude. When they fail to obey, they can thank God that their relationship with him isn't predicated upon their obedience but upon Jesus's obedience. Even their disobedience can be an occasion to remind them their Savior is praying for them and their sin won't ever separate them from him or his love for them. He continues to smile at them because they are his beloved children, with whom he is well pleased.

Jesus's Righteousness Establishes Our Goodness

Let's visit that colorful playroom again with Joshua, Jordan, and Caleb. Today, instead of learning about Jonah, they're studying the Ten Commandments. The lesson calls for making two tablets that look like the stone tablets God wrote his perfect law upon (Exod. 20). Cardboard, foil, scissors, and a permanent marker illustrate the demands of God's beautiful law.

The three brothers are instructed to consider every one of the laws and rehearse how they've failed to obey them. They take the permanent marker and write their name by each one, and read about the blessings and curses for obedience and disobedience in Deuteronomy 28–29.

Their mother says,

God demands perfect obedience to his law, children, but that's not all he's done. Let me read you something else that's so exciting, from Colossians 2:13–14. "When you were dead in your sins and in the uncircumcision of your flesh, God made you alive with Christ. He forgave us all our sins, having canceled the charge of our legal indebtedness, which stood against us and condemned us; he has taken it away, nailing it to the cross." When we look at the Ten Commandments, it's obvious we have a record of doing wrong. We fail to be good. But this Scripture tells us this record of wrongdoing was nailed to the cross when Christ died.

Leaving the playroom, the family then goes outside, carrying their "stone" tablets. Each one of the boys picks up a wooden cross their mom made earlier and, using a hammer and nails, they cover the record of their disobedience with the wooden cross.

Their mom continues,

> Your record of disobedience is only covered up by the cross if you trust in Jesus as your Rescuer. If you know that you cannot obey these commandments no matter how hard you try, and if you know that you need someone to obey them for you, Jesus Christ is that Somebody. The Bible says he's your righteousness (1 Cor. 1:30). He makes you truly good inside and out. And he helps you to obey.
>
> But if you don't care about the commandments, or you're trying to obey them to make God love you, it unfortunately won't work. This terrible debt of disobedience is all you have to offer to the holy Creator of everything—and he loves you regardless. So, let's pray God opens your eyes to his law and the good news that he can rescue you, and that you'll receive his grace for you.

Raising good kids is utterly impossible unless they are drawn by the Holy Spirit to put their faith in the goodness of Jesus, and you cannot be a good parent on your own either. There is only one Good Parent, and he has one Good Son. Together this Father and Son have accomplished everything needed to rescue us and our children from certain destruction. When we put our faith in him, he bestows the benediction upon us all: "These are my beloved children, in whom I am well pleased."

Remembering God's Grace

As we learn to give our children grace, we need to remind ourselves of the gospel, too, and remember how much we need God's grace as well. Slow down and take a moment to reflect on these questions and engage with the Holy Spirit.

1) How can you encourage your kids when they are obedient and point them to the goodness of Jesus?

2) In what ways are "human obedience" and "passive righteousness" different? In what ways do you try to make them the same?

3) How does teaching your children about justification and Christ's righteousness help them to become truly good?

Raising Our Kids by Faith and Grace Alone

The law says, "Do this," and it is never done. Grace says, "Believe in this," and everything is already done.

Martin Luther[1]

Our family has annual passes to the Disneyland and California Adventure theme parks, so we happily make the drive up I-5 several times a year to spend the day screaming and laughing and racing from ride to ride. One of the rides that terrifies us most is Mickey's Fun Wheel, a 150-foot-tall Ferris wheel. Now, before you roll your eyes about our being scared of a Ferris wheel, let me tell you a little more. Like most Ferris wheels, you enter a gondola or cage at the bottom of the wheel (while other people are screaming in terror at the top). Then you're lifted up and the real "fun" begins. You see, Mickey's Fun Wheel is actually a ride within a ride. As the cages (and you) are raised by the wheel, they also slide along interior curves so that as the wheel turns, you have the terrifying sensation you're about to plummet down onto the boardwalk below. And, of course, we always have children with us (some older than others) who think it's hysterical to rock the thing as much as they possibly can. Really, we ride all types of roller coasters, and nothing frightens us like this thing. We've concluded that it's so frightening because we can't see where we're going and there is nothing to hang on to. No buckles. No nice, padded harnesses. It's just us and a cage gliding in some unknown pattern 150 feet over Anaheim. We're up there, flapping in the breeze and hoping that whoever welded our gondola together wasn't busy texting their sweetheart when the critical welds were being made.

So far we've given you a paradigm for parenting that might feel a bit like Mickey's Fun Wheel—or maybe it's not that much fun. Your head might be spinning. You might be thinking we've taken all this gospel stuff a bit too far, or you may simply be befuddled and wondering what you're supposed to do now. *Okay, I'll throw away my charts and stickers, but then what? There had better be something else for me to hang on to!*

We understand. We're right there with you, swaying in that gondola with nothing under us but grace. And while we long to be free from the tyrannical misconception that our children's success is entirely up to us, our palms are beginning to get clammy too. Like you, we're very comfortable relying on the rules as the means to achieve our goals. Here's the formula we're most at ease with: *good parenting in, good children out.* Seems easy and comforting, doesn't it? Of course, there's always the question whether or not our parenting will be good enough, but still, our reliance on the law is like standing with feet firmly planted on good old terra firma. (Until, of course, we remember that Southern California is prone to earthquakes, after all.)

Releasing our hold on the law causes us to feel lost and abandoned, just like you might be feeling now. Of course, we don't like the law, but grace just feels terrifying, like swinging in that wretched gondola or free-falling into faith. Trust that God is *that* good? Give up trust in ourselves and our own efforts?

Salvation and Good Parenting Are of the Lord

Jessica and I know you want steps and buckles and padded harnesses. We do too. And it's for this reason we're going to remind you of what we wrote in the introduction: parenting with grace must not be another formula to employ to try to control God and your children. Sure, there are plenty of practical steps you can take with your kids, but fundamentally you'll have to embrace the truth that their salvation and their upbringing are all by grace alone.

Here are a couple of examples of God's grace at work. So far in this book, I have confessed how moralistic my parenting was. My husband, Phil, and I rarely gave our kids the gospel. We were frequently harsh and overly strict. At other times, we were apathetic and self-absorbed. Even so, here I am writing a book on gospel parenting with our daughter, Jessica. There's a lesson in this admission. Salvation is all about grace. Please don't think that I'm being modest or humble. I'm not. Our parenting was completely law-, fear-, and control-driven. Sure, we had fun and we loved each other, but Jesus was nowhere to be found.

In addition, my own childhood was far from ideal. Although my mother loved my brother and me, she was a single parent struggling to provide for us. At times she worked two jobs to try to make ends meet. My brother and I were basically left to raise ourselves alone. During our teen years, my mother also struggled with a debilitating bone disorder that made her even less available to us. We never had family devotions. We never prayed before meals. Unless my grandmother took us to church, we rarely went. Because she was working such long hours, my mother rarely attended any special school functions. As I grew up, I became an angry, selfish, shameless person. But God saved me. He used all the heartache to make me see how great he was and how I needed him. He transformed my heart to love him. And he continues to use all the trouble from my childhood to help me be thankful for grace.

God has been kind to Phil and me, and, of course, his kindness never means any of us should cavalierly ignore our parenting responsibilities and assume God will just save our kids if he wants to. No, to live like that would be unbelieving, disobedient, and presumptuous. We would be failing to love our children and the Lord. We are always to do our best, strive to be obedient as parents, and love, nurture, and correct our kids, but we are to do so with faith in the Lord's ability to transform hearts, not in our own ability to be consistent or faithful. Seeking to be faithfully obedient parents is our responsibility. Granting faith to our children and raising them in grace is his. Freedom to love and enjoy our children flows out of the knowledge that God saves them *in spite of our best efforts*, not because of them.

To put it another way, you might ask yourself, *Well, if that's the truth, why on earth am I working so hard at this? If God really is sovereign and is going to do what he wants to do and save my children with or without me, then why am I beating my brains out? Why am I not on a cruise somewhere enjoying life instead of reading this book?*

When confronted with God's merciful sovereignty, a sovereignty that will use both faithful and unfaithful parenting as the means to draw children to himself, the propensity to give up in apathy is very strong. We pride ourselves in being self-reliant. We want to work and get paid a guaranteed wage. So when we're not promised a reward, we think we shouldn't have to work. This thinking is fallacious because the relationship we have with God isn't one between a master and slave or employer and employee. It's a relationship between a loving Father and his dearly loved daughters and sons.

We don't work toward becoming faithful parents because we want to earn a reward. We don't strive to raise our children well to earn God's blessing. *We work to become the parents God desires us to be because we already have his blessing* (Rom. 4:4–8). We do it because we love him and because he loves us. We do it because we love our children. And we keep going through all the ups and downs of parenting because God may use our efforts as the means to draw our children to him.

So, how can you tell whether your parenting efforts are motivated by reliance on God's grace or by self-trust? How can you know whether you're trying to obligate God or serve him in gratitude? One way to judge is to consider your reaction when your children fail. If you are angry, frustrated, or despairing because you work so hard and they aren't responding, then you're working (at least in part) for the wrong reasons. Conversely, if you're proud when your children obey and get puffed up by receiving those desired kudos—*Oh! Your kids are so good!*—you should suspect your motives. Both pride and despair grow in all our hearts, especially when we are self-reliant.

It's Not All Up to You

So many parents I know would characterize parenting as hard, grinding labor. At times, parents feel like failures. Faithful parenting *is* hard work. That's not what I'm concerned about. I'm concerned about parents who carry the entire burden for their kids' salvation and lifelong happiness on their shoulders. We were never meant to carry the ultimate responsibility for anyone's soul, neither our own nor our children's. Only the Good Shepherd is strong enough to carry a soul. And although that kind of committed parenting appears godly, it is nothing less than works-righteousness and idolatry. Living in grace will bring freedom and joy to you as a parent also.

Works-Righteousness

Works-righteousness is a dangerous and false variation of godly obedience. Godly obedience is motivated by love for God and trust in his gracious plan and power. Works-righteousness is motivated by unbelief. It is a reliance on our own abilities and a desire to control outcomes. It eventuates in penance: *Lord, I'll make it up to you by redoubling my efforts tomorrow!* rather than repentance:

Lord, forgive me for my sin today. Thank you for loving me despite all my failures. In parenting, works-righteousness will cause us to be both fearful and demanding. When we see our own failures, we will be overcome with fear: *I really blew it with my kids today. I'm so afraid that I'm going to ruin them!* When we see their failures, we'll be overly demanding: *I've already told you what I want you to do. Didn't you hear me? I must have told you fifty times in the last five minutes! I'm sick to death of your terrible attitude. You need to listen to me and do what I say without any complaints or grunts or eyerolls! Just do it!* It's obvious how both of these responses feed off each other in a never-ending cycle of anger and despair and penance.

Works-righteousness obliterates the sweet comforts of grace because it cuts us off from God, who *alone* is the giver of grace. It cuts us off because he absolutely insists on being our sole Savior. This is his claim: "I, even I, am the LORD, and *apart from me there is no savior*" (Isa. 43:11; see also 45:21). This is important enough to bear repeating: we are not nor can we be the saviors of our children. God is the Savior. When we forget this, our parenting will be pockmarked by fear, severity, and exhaustion.

On the other hand, when we rest in his gracious work and love, we will experience the comforts he provides for us. He delights in being worshiped as the one "who richly provides us with everything for our enjoyment" (1 Tim. 6:17). And he loves flooding our consciences with the peace that comes from knowing our sins are forgiven and our standing before him is completely secure. When we're quietly resting in grace, we'll have grace to give our children too. When we're freed from the ultimate responsibility of being their savior, we'll find our parenting burden becoming easier and lighter.

> Are you tired? Worn out? Burned out on religion? Come to me. Get away with me and you'll recover your life. I'll show you how to take a real rest. Walk with me and work with me—watch how

I do it. Learn the unforced rhythms of grace. I won't lay anything heavy or ill-fitting on you. Keep company with me and you'll learn to live freely and lightly. (Matt. 11:28–30 MSG)

Idolatry

Simply speaking, idolatry is worshiping and serving any other god but God. We all struggle with idolatry. Within the heart of the Christian, idolatry is frequently the worship of some good, like having believing, obedient children. This desire is not sinful or idolatrous in itself. It is good. But it becomes idolatrous when we orient our entire lives around it or sin because we want it too much. When we so desperately want our children to be good that we become angry, fearful, proud, or sullen, then our desire for their transformation has become the god we serve. Yes, God does command us to train our children, but care needs to be taken that this training doesn't morph into something more important to us than God himself. Remember that Abraham was commended by God for being willing to sacrifice his son in worship to him (Gen. 22:15–17). Jesus also echoed this same truth when he uttered this shocking statement:

> If anyone comes to me and does not hate father and mother, wife *and children*, brothers and sisters—yes, even their own life—such a person cannot be my disciple. (Luke 14:26)

Idolatry is always subject to the law of diminishing returns too. In other words, our children's obedience today is never quite good enough tomorrow. I've also counseled with parents whose children were godly and faithful, but they were dissatisfied with them because the children didn't live up to some sort of preconceived notion the parent held. If you've ever wondered why you seem to be so demanding and why "good" is never "good enough" for you, perhaps idolatry is the answer. Perhaps you once heard that successful parenting meant that your children would always obey the first time they were told and with a smiling face. As with every other form of idolatry, parents perform the prescribed rituals and expect the desired results. *Good parenting in, good kids out.* But then, when our children refuse to satisfy our desires, we feel devastated. *But I worked so hard and tried to do everything right! What happened?*

Our idolatry is a symptom of a deeper problem: unbelief. We raise our kids' success and our parenting techniques to the status of godhood because we simply don't believe God is good enough to trust with our children's souls or wise enough to know what will make us ultimately happy and satisfied. *We have far too high a view of our own ability to shape our children and far too low a view of God's love and trustworthiness.* So we multiply techniques and try to control the outcome. We subconsciously hope that by our "righteousness" we will obligate God to make everything turn out the way we want. Honestly, it's no wonder that all the parents sitting around the park with their kids need a nap so badly. Idolatry, like all sin, is devastating to the soul. It cuts us off from the comforts of grace, the peace of conscience, and the joy that is to be our strength.

Grace for the Meltdown

One day, when Wesley was four or so, Jessica remembers sitting in the park with a new friend we'll call Catherine. Catherine was new to Christianity and new in our church. Like all moms do at parks, they began a conversation about their children. The conversation turned to the subject of how to raise children. Jessica tried to explain to Catherine how important biblical, consistent, loving discipline was. She talked glowingly about how beneficial it was in little Wesley's life.

But then, when it was time to leave, Wesley decided he didn't want to go. Apparently, it was against his plan for eternal happiness. So he threw himself to the ground in the parking lot and had a fit. Jessica felt humiliated. Everything she had just said to Catherine was flying right back in her face.

Jessica struggled with her own works-righteousness. She felt fearful and angry. She also struggled with her desire for her new friend to think well of her and her parenting methods. She wondered, *What does she think of me now? What does she think of my son?* She started making excuses: "He normally doesn't act this way." By the time she got Wesley buckled in the car, she was consumed with her own failure as a parent. *I do exactly what the Bible says, so why isn't God helping me or changing my child? I'll never talk about parenting to anyone ever again!*

If Jessica had remembered in that moment to parent in light of grace, she could have responded differently. Knowing the character of her heavenly Father, she could have remembered that every time something unexpected happens, it is God once again approaching her in love to show her the glories of the gospel and the beauties of grace. She could have been reminded that correction doesn't transform the soul; only Jesus Christ does. When she saw Wesley lying there, throwing a fit, she could have seen a picture of her own heart. She could have heard the Lord remind her that this rebel heart was just like her own. The Lord might have spoken to her heart like this:

> This is you. This is what your heart is like outside of my grace. You're no different. This is just another opportunity for you to delight in my goodness to you. Do you see how angry you are? Do you see how you need me? You're ashamed because Wesley is acting this way in front of a friend you're hoping to impress. But my Son is not ashamed to call you sister (Heb. 2:11). You're focusing on your reputation because you think friendship with Catherine will make you happy. You're forgetting that I am the source of your happiness. Wesley is helping me show you how much you need a Savior too. You and Wesley are just alike. You're both sinful, but you're both loved. Neither of you has earned my love, but I've graciously bestowed it upon you.

Then, without idolatry, works-righteousness, or unbelief, Jessica could have disciplined Wesley after he cooled down with these words:

> Sweetheart, I love you. When I tell you it is time to go, we must leave. I know you don't want to go, but when we don't get what we want, it isn't okay to start screaming and throw ourselves to the ground. There are two things you have to understand. First, you were being unsafe. God has put me in charge of you, and I'm responsible to keep you safe. When you lie in a parking lot with cars around, you could get hurt. So when I tell you to come, I am doing what I believe will keep you safe. Second, when you don't listen and obey, you are sinning against God and against me. I understand that you didn't want to leave the park. I know how difficult it is to show control when you don't get what you want. And because you can't control yourself, you need Jesus. Do you know what he did when he had to go somewhere he didn't want to go? He told God that he would do whatever God wanted him to do. He did that for you, and he did that for me. The place he didn't want to go was the cross. He knew the cross was going to be hard, and it would hurt him a lot. But he did what he didn't want to do because he loves us. Also, I want you to know that you're not the only one being corrected today. Today God showed me his love by correcting me too. He showed me how I was being angry in my heart too. He showed me my own brokenness. Times of correction are painful, but I have faith that God will use today in both of our lives to make us love him more.

Faith in God's Gracious Sovereignty

Elyse and I (Jessica) want to free you from the unbelief and works-righteousness that rob you of the comforts of grace. We want your parenting, though it seems difficult and never-ending, to be free from idolatry and unbelief. We want to encourage you to live by faith in the Son of God who loved you and gave himself for you (Gal. 2:20), not by your own efforts.

Yes, parents are to be faithful and diligent. But even so, there are no promises in the Bible that even our best grace-based parenting will produce believing, behaving children. None. Even if we parent according to grace, there are no guarantees. As my children have grown into adulthood, I have been reminded of this over and over again. The beautifully comforting thought, though, is that God is still with us, working, loving, and training us to trust in him.

When we think about it, there are very few examples of godly parents producing godly children in the Bible. Consider the Old Testament saints who are known for serving the Lord. Abraham wasn't raised in a godly home—his father was an idolater. Joseph's dad sinfully favored him and disrespected his brothers because their mother wasn't as pretty as Joseph's mother. Moses was raised by an unmarried woman who worshiped the sun. David's dad thought so little of him that he didn't remember to include him when Samuel came looking for Israel's next king. Daniel's parents were idolaters and were judged by God in the exile.

What we do see in the Bible are examples of children who had terribly wicked parents but ended up serving the Lord faithfully. King Hezekiah is a good illustration of this. He was the son of one of the wickedest kings in Judah, King Ahaz, but Hezekiah wasn't ruined by his father's wickedness. Instead, Hezekiah is famous for his faith and allegiance to the Lord. But then Hezekiah had a son named Manasseh who "led Judah and the people of Jerusalem astray, so that they did more evil than the nations the LORD had destroyed before the Israelites" (2 Chron. 33:9), and Manasseh had a wicked son named Amon—but Amon had a righteous son named Josiah. There's a message for us in this lineage: righteous parents do not necessarily produce righteous children. Wicked parents do not necessarily produce wicked children. It seems rather as though God delights in saving the children of his enemies. God delights in doing what we cannot do. He alone is Savior.

Timothy, in the New Testament, had a believing mother and grandmother who taught him the Scriptures and gave him a good foundation (2 Tim. 1:5; 3:15). However, he also had an unbelieving father (Acts 16:1–3). Timothy's dad wasn't an engaged, gospel-preaching, devotion-leading, righteous man. He wasn't a believer at all. So God brought Paul to be a father to Timothy. Timothy fulfilled God's sovereign purpose by being a son to Paul, and Paul fulfilled God's purpose in being a father for Timothy. Parents who have unbelieving or disengaged spouses should rest in this truth and never fear that their spouse's unbelief will close the doors of the kingdom to their children.

Furthermore, no one in the first churches was raised in gospel-centered homes. In fact, when we study the cultures in Corinth, Ephesus, or Rome, where infanticide was a normal practice and children were considered chattel, we should wonder that the early church was populated at all. No one in Jerusalem knew any secrets to successful parenting that would help their children have faith in the Messiah, but the church was established anyway. That's because God can do all things, and no purpose of his can be thwarted (Job 42:2).

Some of you raised in the church may be thinking, *But what about Proverbs 22:6? "Start children off on the way they should go, and even when they are old they will not turn from it." Doesn't that verse teach that if we train our children in the right path, they will not depart from our training?*

Understanding this verse begins with understanding the kind of literature it is. The book of Proverbs isn't comprised of conditional promises but rather maxims or wise sayings. They describe, in a general sense, the way that God makes the world run. But there are plenty of examples where it's obvious that these maxims don't hold true all the time. Proverbs 10:4 is just one example: "Lazy hands make for poverty, but diligent hands bring wealth." While it is generally true that hard work produces wealth, it's not always the case. There are plenty of hardworking parents or families who don't have the privilege of generational wealth and single parents who work multiple jobs and still only barely make rent. Another example is found in the proverb about the virtuous woman: "Her children arise and call her blessed; her husband also, and he praises her" (31:28). How many virtuous women have been scorned by children and husband only to be welcomed and honored by the Lord? Thousands? Millions?

When we fail to understand this form of literature and build our lives on an incorrect interpretation of it, we end up with a philosophy akin to that of Job's comforters. They had a very simple formula for obtaining God's blessing: *go and do the right thing.* Conversely, they believed that if you didn't have God's outward blessing, it must be because you weren't doing what he wanted you to do. They thought faithful obedience always obligated God to respond in the way they desired. They were wrong (Job 42:7–8).

While it is true that God may grace wise parents with godly children, that is not always the case. God may use your parenting as a means to draw your children to himself. He may use other means and at a different time. Or he may use a child's rebellion and disinterest as a way to accomplish his unexpected will. Nothing we can do puts a lock on God blessing us in the way we expect.

The Path of Faith

Why doesn't God give us a sure promise that if we parent well our children will do well? Wouldn't our parenting be more consistent if we thought we had the ability to save them? No, it actually wouldn't. We wouldn't work harder if we had that command and promise because we don't respond well to commands. True obedience doesn't come from commands combined with promises. The nation of Israel and their response to Deuteronomy 28–29 ought to be enough proof of that.

God doesn't promise our children's salvation in response to our obedience because he never encourages self-reliance. It would be against God's character to give us a promise that our children will be saved if we raise them in a certain way. That would mean he was telling us to trust in something other than Christ's grace and mercy. He would be encouraging us to trust in ourselves, and God never does that. The way of the Lord is always a way of faith—faith in his goodness, mercy, and love.

So, here's our hope: before time began, God the Father saw each of us, individually and distinctly. He not only saw us, he *knew* us. This means he was intimately acquainted with everything about us before we even existed. He chose us to be in relationship with him, for us to be his children. But he didn't do this because of any good he saw in us. All of us have absolutely *nothing* to boast about. He chose us out of his sheer grace and because he loves loving the unlovely. Because of his great love for us, he deserves to be fully loved by us. This means we transfer our entire trust (and keep transferring it over and over again) to him. This is faith. In the same way that you trust in him and not in yourself for your salvation and your parenting, you can trust in him for the salvation and growth of your children. You can give yourself grace: he's in control, he is loving, and his plan is best. And you can give your children grace too.

Parenting with grace isn't another set of rules for you to follow. It's a story you can rejoice in. Share this story with your children. Show them the Savior. Show them Jesus.

Here's Your Step of Faith for the Day: Believe

At one point during Christ's earthly ministry, people came to him looking for a formula for successful living.

> Then they asked him, "What must we do to do the works God requires?" Jesus answered, "The work of God is this: to believe in the one he has sent." (John 6:28–29)

They wanted a list. Can't you just hear their hearts? *Just tell us what to do, and we'll get about it. We know we can, and we really want to, so just give us the list and we'll work it out*. Here was a great opportunity for the Lord to give them the law again. But he knew what they would do with it. He had watched their response to it for thousands of years. He knew what was in their hearts (2:25). No, more rules were not what they needed. They needed faith.

Do you want to do the work of God? Okay, then believe. Believe God is strong enough to save your children no matter how you fail. Believe he is loving enough to bring them all the way into relationship with himself whether you get "grace parenting" or not. And believe he is wise enough to know the right way and the right time to do it. What do you need to do? Simply believe: "Believe in the Lord Jesus, and you will be saved, you and your household" (Acts 16:31; see also Rom. 9:30–32; 10:3–4). In the words of Martin Luther, which we opened this chapter with, "The law says, 'Do this,' and it is never done. Grace says, 'Believe in this,' and everything is already done."[2] Everything is already done. Can you believe that? Will you?

Here's your invitation to take a ride on what might initially feel like Mickey's Fun Wheel in your parenting. All those rules about how to get your kids to "work the works of God" need to be left on the ground outside the gate. Step into the gondola and trust in him alone. Even though the tight buckles and restricting harnesses of the law might feel like welcome security to you, in the end they will chafe, and you'll want to throw them off. The law may serve for a time to keep your kids from rocking the cage too much, but eventually they will chafe against it too. They will look for ways around it. Buckles and harnesses might make you *feel* more secure, but the shocking truth is that they cannot control the direction of the gondola. The same goes for your parenting—you're completely at the mercy of God's love. You don't need to be afraid of it. The gospel teaches us that being at God's mercy is a place of rest and blessing, so wouldn't falling into his merciful arms be a good thing?

The law seems so reassuring, but it is a false assurance. It is only God's grace that is sufficient to sustain and transform us. Grace is stronger than all our work and all our weaknesses, and it is made perfect when we humble ourselves before God's desire to glorify his Son and not our great parenting (2 Cor. 12:9). Salvation is of the Lord. He is our Rescuer, our Helper, our Perfect Parent. Climb aboard and have a seat. No buckles here, just faith. Your loving Father has things well in hand. Believe. Live in freedom and joy.

Remembering God's Grace

1) In what ways do you idolize having "good" kids?

2) How is the formula of "Good parenting in, good children out" contrary to the gospel?

3) How would resting in God's goodness change your relationship with your children?

4

Jesus Loves All His Little Prodigals and Pharisees

One can be addicted to either lawlessness or lawfulness. Theologically there is no difference since both break relationship with God, the giver.

Gerhard O. Forde[1]

Sparkling blue water and warm summer breezes mean school's finally out, and Brenda's kids, Susan and David, are living at the pool. Today, all the neighborhood children are enjoying a fine game of Marco Polo.

While overseeing the game and watching for their safety, Brenda tries to grab a few rays of sunshine for herself. But then, with chagrin, she notices the tone of the game has started to change. Groaning to herself, she thinks, *Here we go again! Why can't I have just one afternoon of rest without them fighting?*

"I quit!" David yells as he climbs out of the pool.

"You're such a cheater!" Susan retorts.

And those are just their beginning volleys. Feeling her own anger beginning to build, Brenda quickly prays, *God, help me believe that this is you approaching me with grace. Please help me see and help me overcome my desire to be left alone. Give me wisdom in parenting my kids right now.*

Calling David and Susan to come to her, she welcomes them both into her arms. Both of them know what's coming, and their hard little faces reflect hearts determined not to listen.

David, younger than Susan by two years, regularly cheats at games to try to give himself an edge over his sister. David is a rulebreaker who rationalizes that cheating is okay because he's littler, and it's not fair that he loses all the time.

"David, I understand why you cheat when you play games. I know that you want to win, but breaking rules, even the rules of a game like Marco Polo, is wrong."

Surprisingly, David replies, "I know, and I'm sorry."

Brenda doubts his "sorry" means anything more than, "Can we be done with this so I can get back into the pool?" but she decides to let him be for now and turns to talk with her little rule-keeper, Susan.

Brenda sees the hardness in her eyes and asks if screaming at her little brother was a kind thing to do.

Susan's response is a sullen no. But then the justification for her anger comes rushing out. "But he always cheats! And then when we tell him to follow the rules, he always quits!"

Brenda knows it's true and that Susan rarely cheated, primarily because she usually won without much effort. Brenda prays for grace because she knows Susan is right but also because she is tired of the continual conflict. *Lord,* she prays, *help me know what to say now. Help me not to give in to my own unbelief or my own efforts, and help me to see you here.*

"Susan," Brenda begins, "I agree with you. David should follow the rules. And I agree that we should remind him to do so." *What now? Something's missing here. Help me, Lord, please.* Then the gospel comes rushing in on a tidal wave of grace. "David should follow the rules of the game, but the rules are not the most important thing. There is something more important than the rules of Marco Polo. Mercy is more important than obeying the rules."

This message confounds Susan, and a questioning look spreads over her face. Even at age nine, she's pretty much figured out that rules and law-keeping are the be-all, end-all. She knows rules are what makes you stay "right," and she loves feeling "right."

"Do you understand how mercy is more important than keeping the rules?" Brenda asks.

Susan shakes her head no. After all, what could be more important than keeping the rules and doing things the right way?

"Susan, let me tell you about something called the law of love."

"The law of love?" she asks. For the first time Susan's face and voice soften. Brenda begins to hope that the Holy Spirit is working in Susan's heart.

"Yes! The law of love is the law that Christ kept perfectly on your behalf. We are all law-breaking rule-haters when it comes to things we want to do. David breaks the rules by cheating, you break the rules by screaming at him, and I break the rules by becoming frustrated and angry at you both. None of us keep the rules or love each other like we should. But when Jesus came, instead of making us pay for breaking the rules, he loved us. Do you know how he loved us?"

Susan knows the answer to this one. "By dying for our sin?"

"Yes, that is right! He took the punishment for our sin to show us that something is more important than rules. Do you know what's more important? It is faith working though love like Galatians 5:6 says: 'For in Christ Jesus neither circumcision nor uncircumcision has any value. The only thing that counts is faith expressing itself through love.' Our keeping the rules or not keeping the rules doesn't really count for anything before God. The only thing that counts is belief that Jesus died for us and, after that, responding in love for God and each other.

"So, you see, Susan, if you truly believe Jesus died for your sin, you can love your rule-breaking little brother. After all, you are just like him. And when you fail to love him, you can remember that Jesus, the Lord of Love, has obeyed the law of love for you and has given his goodness to you. And then, because of how beautiful he is, and how beautiful his love for you is, you can get back in the water and play, remembering that loving your brother the way Christ loved you is more important than following the rules of Marco Polo."

Susan goes back to the pool, and her softness changes David's attitude and posture toward his sister. Brenda looks at both of them with love and understanding. They're beginning to comprehend the good news.

Within every household—and even within every person—there is a Susan and a David. There are those who love to think they're keeping the rules and those who don't care about the rules as much as they care about other things like winning or having a good time. The heart of a Susan and a David resides within each of us, and who shows up simply depends on what's at stake on any given day. Do we want to win? Do we want to claim the moral high ground? Welcome, Susan and David. The law doesn't transform the heart of either. It only makes them proud if they obey or throw their hands up in sad frustration. The only power strong enough to transform the selfishly rebellious and the selfishly self-righteous is grace.

The Welcoming Father

A story of grace we love, and that many of us might be familiar with, is the story Jesus told in Luke 15:11–32.

> There was a man who had two sons. The younger one said to his father, "Father, give me my share of the estate." So he divided his property between them.
> Not long after that, the younger son got together all he had, set off for a distant country and there squandered his wealth in wild

living. After he had spent everything, there was a severe famine in that whole country, and he began to be in need. So he went and hired himself out to a citizen of that country, who sent him to his fields to feed pigs. He longed to fill his stomach with the pods that the pigs were eating, but no one gave him anything.

When he came to his senses, he said, "How many of my father's hired servants have food to spare, and here I am starving to death! I will set out and go back to my father and say to him: Father, I have sinned against heaven and against you. I am no longer worthy to be called your son; make me like one of your hired servants." So he got up and went to his father.

But while he was still a long way off, his father saw him and was filled with compassion for him; he ran to his son, threw his arms around him and kissed him.

The son said to him, "Father, I have sinned against heaven and against you. I am no longer worthy to be called your son."

But the father said to his servants, "Quick! Bring the best robe and put it on him. Put a ring on his finger and sandals on his feet. Bring the fattened calf and kill it. Let's have a feast and celebrate. For this son of mine was dead and is alive again; he was lost and is found." So they began to celebrate.

Meanwhile, the older son was in the field. When he came near the house, he heard music and dancing. So he called one of the servants and asked him what was going on. "Your brother has come," he replied, "and your father has killed the fattened calf because he has him back safe and sound."

The older brother became angry and refused to go in. So his father went out and pleaded with him. But he answered his father, "Look! All these years I've been slaving for you and never disobeyed your orders. Yet you never gave me even a young goat so I could celebrate with my friends. But when this son of yours who has squandered your property with prostitutes comes home, you kill the fattened calf for him!"

"My son," the father said, "you are always with me, and everything I have is yours. But we had to celebrate and be glad, because this brother of yours was dead and is alive again; he was lost and is found."

Although this story is usually known as the parable of the prodigal son, a better name for it might be something like the parable of the welcoming father. Why? Because its astounding lesson is that an utterly good father welcomes two sons who are outwardly very different but inwardly exactly the same.

One of the sons is like our little David: tired of being youngest, anxious to prove his manhood, cavalier about the rules. He sets out with his inheritance to free himself from the shadow of his brother's crushing goodness. And he accomplishes his goal. He slides from an elevated place of status and position in the community down to a pig trough. He thoroughly degrades himself; he is desolate, starving, and desperate for rescue.

The other son is like our Susan. He loves feeling right and prides himself on keeping the rules. And now that his brother has left, he really relishes the fact that he has won the battle of "best son." He feels he has finally and fully secured all his father's blessing.

If your parenting is moralistic, like most of ours, children like David will break your heart but Susan will make you proud. It is only when you parent with grace that the complete need of both children becomes apparent. Children who embarrass you and children who make you proud must both be taught the deeper truth of the welcoming father—that mercy trumps law.

So, although the two sons are integral to the story, they aren't the main characters. No, the main character in this story is the father who joyfully welcomes both his sons to his table. Hear the father's heart in Christ's description of his welcome of the younger son: "But while he was still a long way off, his father saw him and was filled with compassion for him; he ran to his son, threw his arms around him and kissed him" (v. 20). The father warmly embraces his smelly, destitute, gaunt son, and the first thing he does is reestablish his place in the family. He renews relationship. He gives him the ring, the robe, the feast.

The "Susans" of the world are not hoping for their errant brother's return. No, of course not. They're out working. And they are filled with proud resentment at the father's welcome home party for his son. But what is the father's response to such arrogance? "So his father went out and pleaded with him" (v. 28). The father's arms are open wide. "You are always with me, and everything I have is yours" (v. 31).

The father's loving welcome extends to both sons, although neither is worthy or deserving in any way. The father has a higher rule, a greater law: merciful love. Our children, both the "bad" ones and the "good" ones, need to hear his message of entreaty: "My arms are open to you; all that is mine is yours. Come and delight in my generous mercy."

Begrudge God's Generosity? Who Would Do That?

At the end of another parable about disgruntled laborers in a vineyard (Matt. 20:1–16), Jesus poses two penetrating questions: "Don't I have the right to do what I want with my own money? Or are you envious because I am generous?" (v. 15). None of us would ever say that we resent God's generous mercy, would we? When we stop and consider our salvation, we're filled with gratitude for his generosity. We know we've been saved by grace alone through faith alone.

But has that gratitude for grace made it all the way down into the way we raise our children? Could it be that in our parenting we act as though God should play by our rules? Do we believe he is obligated to bestow his gifts in a way that coincides with our sense of right and wrong? Here's how this mistake may play out in our foundational beliefs: we're very comfortable with thinking, *Good parenting in, good children out*, which then translates to our children with this maxim: "Good behavior in, God's smile out."

This is the mistake the disgruntled laborers in the parable make. They think there should be a one-for-one correlation between their work and the master's reward. Then, when the master refuses to acquiesce to their expectations, they become envious and angry.

The problem, of course, is that God is not a cosmic vending machine (assuming we've got enough quarters to make any difference to him!), nor should we be dictators of how he dispenses his grace. His mercy always goes beyond what we deem is fair, and his grace extends further than we can imagine.

The Gospel Is for Sinners

So, how can we teach our children to rejoice in and receive God's generous mercy and love? We know we need to train them in rules for obedience; that's obvious. But how can we teach them about something as outside of the norm as God's joy in being merciful to sinners?

The first way we do that is to see and confess our own propensities to live like one of the two sons. Confess to your David that you, too, break the rules and always justify yourself for doing so. Confess to your Susan that you, too, love to rely on the rules and feel superior to others.

Being specific about the ways you are simultaneously proud and disobedient will help your children understand that the gospel is for everyone and everyone is a sinner who needs grace. The gospel is not good news to those who pride themselves on their hard work. It is infuriating news. But it is good news to younger brother types who are tempted to turn away from the faith early on because they don't think the gospel is for sinners. They think it is for good people who like being "gooder." Consistent, transparent, and specific confession of sin will help them see how their parents struggle with sin in the same ways they do.

This dynamic is especially important if there is a highly successful elder brother type in the home. Teaching David that he and Susan and Mom are all lost, all sick, and all in need of salvation is so very crucial. On the other hand, saying things like, "Why can't you be more like Susan?" obliterates the gospel message and tells David there is something intrinsically wrong with him that isn't wrong with Susan. It destroys his hope of ever hearing God's proclamation of goodness over his life and breeds unbelief and despair. And it is false. God finds great joy in welcoming Davids to his table. And because they feel their lostness so keenly, they may more easily recognize their need for a Rescuer. Their lives are usually messier and more dramatic, but they also can be more authentic, as Davids can be inspired to turn their lives around because they know they've been forgiven for so much.

As much as David needs to hear about your struggle with sin, Susan needs it even more. She's usually the parent-pleaser who honestly enjoys making you happy and thinks your happiness and God's are analogous. What she desperately needs is to realize that her parents still struggle with sin even though the gospel has made them love holiness. Specific confession of pride, judgment, criticism, envy, and selfish ambition will help Susan understand her own propensities to fail in the same ways—but praising Susan for being a "good girl" will breed toxic pride in her heart. It will teach her that she isn't all that bad, and she won't recognize her need for a Rescuer. What do Susans need to hear? They need to hear that they don't need to prove their worthiness or goodness because Christ has done the work and fulfilled all the rules for them. They just need to believe and receive it.

Of course, our confession of sin is to be moderated by wisdom. For instance, we never want to confess to our children that we don't really like them very much or we wish they had never been born. This kind of information will not bless them with freedom to admit their own sinfulness or trust us. In addition, we should be careful about the categories of sin we confess. There are certain sins children can't understand or are private matters between the adults in the family. A good rule for confession is that it is appropriate to confess any sin the child has become aware of or any sin that has affected them personally. For instance, if you've been sinfully angry because your children interrupted your time by the pool, you can fully disclose your heart to them and ask them for forgiveness and for prayer. When they overhear you speaking in a proud, unkind way about someone, you can confess that too.

Most parents know enough to confess their anger to their children. But do we regularly confess our self-righteousness and pride? Saying something to them like, "I can't believe you would do something like that!" or showing them a slight coldness combined with a disapproving look should be followed by, "Please forgive me for forgetting that you and I are just the same. We both sin. When I say things like that, I am being self-righteous and forgetting Jesus had to die for my sins too. I'm sure my words hurt you, but that's not all. They were also against the truth of the gospel. I hope you can forgive me. Let's pray that the Lord will help us both to be humble and thankful for grace."

Calling All Sinners

In the following narrative, we see both a Susan and a David. How does the Savior comfort and confront each one?

> While Jesus was having dinner at Matthew's house, many tax collectors and sinners came and ate with him and his disciples. When the Pharisees saw this, they asked his disciples, "Why does your teacher eat with tax collectors and sinners?"
>
> On hearing this, Jesus said, "It is not the healthy who need a doctor, but the sick. But go and learn what this means: 'I desire mercy, not sacrifice.' For I have not come to call the righteous, but sinners." (Matt. 9:10–13)

Echoing the prophet Hosea, Jesus flips everything in our quid pro quo world on its head. Instead of commending those who are outwardly good, he demeans them and sends them back to school. Although they pride themselves on being good and obeying the law, they completely misread God's nature and purpose. This ignorance has calcified their hearts, stripping them of their love for God and blinding them to the needs of their neighbor. They do not see their need of rescue nor that their Rescuer is with them. (Luke 19:44). Only sinners who know they are sinners will hear the word *mercy* spoken over them. Susans and Davids need to know they are sinners (or saved but still struggle with sin), the gospel is for sinners, and there is a Rescuer who loves pouring out mercy on those who cannot help themselves.

Give grace to your children today by teaching them about sin and mercy. Tell your Susans they can relax into God's loving embrace and stop thinking they have to perform in order to get their welcoming Father to love them. Tell your Davids they can have hope and, even though they really struggle, they are the very sort of people Jesus loves being around.

It's obvious how easy it is for us parents to be both prodigals and Pharisees—and on the same day! For instance, we're apathetic when we'd rather sit by the pool and just give the kids a time-out when they fight, or better yet just ignore them and hope they work it out on their own. *Who wants to take time to talk about anything? They never listen anyway. When is it my day to rest?*

On the other hand, we're demanding rule-keepers when we take God's law and incessantly whack our kids over the head with it. "God says you must be honest and never cheat. I can't believe you would sin like that! Don't you know that cheating is like lying, and liars go to hell?" Or "Susan, you're always so unkind. I think you need to memorize that passage from Ephesians 4 about kindness again. Go do it and then come and tell me when you're truly sorry. But first, go apologize to your brother."

What's truly amazing is that Jesus Christ loves both rule-breakers and rule-keepers. And he wants them to be filled with joy and freedom. Because of the Son's perfect obedience, both Susans and Davids can be called "Beloved." When the believing rule-breaker sins, he can look up and say, "Jesus is my righteousness." And when the believing rule-keeper realizes her self-righteousness, she too can look up and say, "Jesus is my righteousness."

And Do Not Hinder Them

I (Elyse) used to sit together on the bench swing with my grand-kids, cozying up under our lap blankets, and we'd sing. We would sing many songs, but the one that we loved best was,

> Jesus loves me, this I know,
> For the Bible tells me so.
> Little ones to him belong,
> They are weak, but he is strong.[2]

What a comfort it is to rest in the knowledge that although we are weak, his love is strong enough to welcome us right up onto his lap. Here is the precious passage where we get a glimpse of this sweet love:

> People were bringing little children to Jesus for him to place his hands on them, but the disciples rebuked them. When Jesus saw this, he was indignant. He said to them, "Let the little children come to me, and do not hinder them, for the kingdom of God belongs to such as these. Truly I tell you, anyone who will not receive the kingdom of God like a little child will never enter it." And he took the children in his arms, placed his hands on them and blessed them. (Mark 10:13–16)

Can't you just imagine this scene? Here are the disciples, filled with ambition and self-righteousness. Children? Women bringing children? Oh, no. Children aren't really important in the grand scheme of things. They haven't learned all we know about how to get in good with God. Climb up on Jesus's lap? Never!

The disciples have failed to understand the heart of what Jesus is teaching them. Like the religious leaders, like the elder brother, like Susan, like most of us, they assume that being important, grown-up, responsible, and good are the ways to get close to God. They're wrong. Can't you see their shock and wonder when Jesus opens his arms and pulls the little ones up onto his lap? He listens to their stories. He draws them close. He smiles warmly. He laughs at their jokes. They have nothing to offer, nothing to give to him. All they have is merely themselves in all their childlike, simple love. They love him because he loves them. And his love is all they need.

Jesus is indignant with his disciples for trying to hinder the children from coming to him. How do we hinder children from coming to the Lord? We get a clue when we look at the context of this story, sandwiched as it is between two others. The first one is about the Pharisee and the tax collector who both go up to pray. Luke tells us that the point of this parable is that some people trust in themselves to be righteous while treating others with contempt, and others bring only a plea for mercy—a plea that is quickly answered.

> But the tax collector stood at a distance. He would not even look up to heaven, but beat his breast and said, "God, have mercy on me, a sinner."
> I tell you that this man, rather than the other, went home justified before God. For all those who exalt themselves will be humbled, and those who humble themselves will be exalted. (Luke 18:13–14)

We hinder our children from enjoying God's embrace when we teach them that their religious activity and obedience elevate them out of the category of sinners in need of mercy. This is the attitude of both the disciples and the religious leaders. Women, children, sinners, Gentiles, differently abled, and the poor are all marginalized and considered insignificant by their society. Yet it is just those sorts of people the Lord loves to draw into his embrace.

We also hinder our children from coming to him when we inadvertently teach them that the good news is meant for people who act good and act right. The story that follows Jesus's encounter with these moms and kids is about a rich, young ruler who has done everything his father had told him. He's a good boy now grown into a "good" man. He's the quintessential elder brother who wants to add Jesus's good teaching to his portfolio. He thinks he can do the works of God and be saved. Even so, we can tell he has a niggling sense that he still isn't quite right or good because he comes to Jesus looking for advice on eternal life. Keepers of the law *never* have full assurance because they know their own hearts. Deep down, hidden away in a locked closet, is the truth that he has never perfectly obeyed. Will he be able to see past his self-righteousness into mercy?

We read his story in Luke 18. Approaching Jesus with the blessed benediction, he asks him, "Good Teacher, what must I do to inherit eternal life?" (v. 18). Dismissing the contradiction between wages and an inheritance, Jesus poses a deeper question: "Why do you call me good? . . . No one is good—except God alone" (v. 19). Jesus begins confronting his self-trust by asking him in so many words, *Are you saying that I am God? Do you know that you aren't good?* The Lord then recites five of the Ten Commandments, to which this young man replies, "All these I have kept since I was a boy" (v. 21). Imagine that. This young man really does think he is good. He has never taken something that belonged to someone else, he has never lied, and he has always honored his parents. What a résumé! Of course, Jesus purposely skips the laws about worship, false gods, and coveting, preferring instead to allow this young ruler time to think.

Then Jesus swings God's hammer, and the death blow is dealt: "You still lack one thing. Sell everything you have and give to the poor, and you will have treasure in heaven. Then come, follow me" (v. 22).

In less than one minute, Jesus annihilates decades of punctilious law-keeping. *There's only one small problem, you see. You don't love your neighbor and you don't love God. You love your goodness, power, and riches. You think you're good, but you're actually bankrupt and sinful.* Jesus knowingly commands him to do something he is unwilling and unable to do. This man can no more renounce what he loves than a camel can go through the eye of a needle. Jesus loves him and wants to peel away his self-trust. Our dear young man's response? "He became very sad, for he was very wealthy" (v. 23).

The response of the people listening in on this incident was utter amazement. *Wow! If this good fellow who has everything going for him and is so religious can't be saved, who can?* In other words, if rich, good people can't make it in, what hope do we have? Who can make it in? Only those who understand they need mercy. Jesus answers, "What is impossible with man is possible with God" (v. 27). God's grace makes it possible for all people to enter into the freedom and wholeness he offers. Those who rely on their own rule keeping are unable to experience the healing they so desperately need. Their eyes are fixed on what they need to do; they don't see what he has done.

With God Nothing Is Impossible

At this point, some of you may be feeling like you've done everything wrong. You might be seeing your errors or are uncomfortably aware that you've missed the message of grace. I want you to know there is hope for you too. So, here's a sip of gospel grace for you to drink in: our children are at the rich mercy of a compassionate God and the atoning work of our perfect representative, Jesus Christ.

When we consistently and unashamedly throw ourselves on God's mercy and teach our children to do the same, we will help them place their hope in him too. We will teach them this hope is "an anchor for the soul, firm and secure" (Heb. 6:19). It is a hope built on "nothing less than Jesus's blood and righteousness . . . [for we] dare not trust the sweetest frame [or attitude] but wholly lean on Jesus's name."[3] We dare not trust even our sweetest efforts or our children's sweetest responses. Instead, we depend utterly on Jesus's name. He is loving. He is good. He is powerful. He's done it all.

As we close this chapter, Jessica and I want to leave you with a comforting message that must never be forgotten: *The disciples couldn't hinder the children from coming to Jesus even though they tried.* When God calls our children to come to him, even if we haven't gotten it all right, even if we've trained little Pharisees or have a house full of prodigals, nothing is impossible for him. He can break through all our flawed methods and redeem all our frail errors. Our society tells us our children's success depends upon our success, but society knows nothing of God's ability to use our failures as a means to bless. "What is impossible with man is possible with God" (Luke 18:27). So, even when we stumble in showing our children mercy, even when we might hinder them from his gracious embrace, Jesus is strong enough to pick each of us up and carry us all the way. Parents, too, are weak—but Jesus is strong. No one, not even you, can thwart his purpose to bless those who are his (Eph. 1:11).

Remembering God's Grace

Take a moment to pause and rest in the goodness of God's grace. Then reflect on the questions below.

1) How have you parented or treated the Susans and Davids in your life? Now, knowing what you've learned in this chapter, how can you apply the gospel and change how you parent/treat them?

2) What can you learn from the story of the welcoming father? How can his posture in loving his two sons teach you to do the same?

_____

_____

3) In what ways have you hindered your children from coming to Jesus? How can you better usher them into Jesus's presence now that you know?

_____

_____

PART 2

Grace in Everyday Parenting

5

Grace That Trains and Nurtures

Grace does not forbid giving directions, promises, corrections and warnings. Only cruelty would forbid such help.

Bryan Chapell[1]

Over the previous chapters, Jessica and I have laid the foundation for why grace is needed in parenting. We've encouraged you to tell your children the message of Christ's love and grace, and when they—and you—forget, to repeat it again and again. This is the blessing of the good news: *Jesus Christ has already done all the work that needed to be done.* When, in great relief from excruciating agony of soul, he declared, "It is finished," it really was. And because of this, we are now empowered to parent with grace from a place of grace.

As we've said, every human heart is drawn to laws and rules, to approval and control. We're tempted to rely on our own strengths, experiences, and what we perceive to be the "right way" to raise children who behave well. But in preaching and living by grace alone, do we disparage rules completely? Does grace negate their necessity? Should we simply ignore our children's behavior and only speak of God's love? Is that what real grace looks like?

Grace That Disciplines

"Grace does not forbid giving directions, promises, corrections and warnings. Only cruelty would forbid such help."[2] Parents are to discipline, instruct, train, and nurture their children. Only a cold detachment, a selfish disdain for a child's desperate need for direction, would cause a parent to refuse to train them. It would be a catastrophic failure if we left them on their own—a complete negation of familial relationship and responsibility.

> If you are not disciplined—and everyone undergoes discipline— then you are not legitimate, not true sons and daughters at all. (Heb. 12:8)

Discipline proves relationship. Instruction demonstrates love. Grace is not averse to training. In fact, one of the functions of grace *is* training in righteousness. Paul shows us how grace trains us:

> For the *grace of God* has appeared, bringing salvation for all people, *training us* to renounce ungodliness and worldly passions, and to live self-controlled, upright, and godly lives in the present age, waiting for our blessed hope, the appearing of the glory of our great God and Savior Jesus Christ, who gave himself for us to redeem us from all lawlessness and to purify for himself a people for his own possession who are zealous for good works. (Titus 2:11–14 ESV)

First, grace trains us by reminding us of all God has already done for us in Christ: he's appeared to us, he's brought us salvation, he's redeemed and purified us, he has promised to return for us, and he's renewing us so we will become like him. It is into this context of gospel truth that training in discipline, or gospel response, is given: because of his great love, we are to renounce ungodliness and worldly passions and live self-controlled, upright, and godly lives. Paul never tires of reminding us of the truth of the gospel. But he also doesn't ignore how we should respond to it. The Holy Spirit teaches us of the glories of Jesus *and* trains us to be holy. Grace trains us to rest in what Christ has done for us *and* to live Christlike lives motivated by the joy and freedom the gospel brings.

All parents, whether they've tasted grace or not, have been given the great privilege and responsibility of being their children's principal teachers. During the first few hours of life, babies are taught by their mothers to trust her to provide for their physical needs. Mom teaches them how to nurse. She swaddles them so they feel warm, secure, loved. As babies grow, if their parents have experienced the life-changing news of the gospel, they will continue to provide for their children and swaddle them in loving discipline as they help them "taste and see that the LORD is good" (Ps. 34:8). It is God's kindness to humankind that he gives children parents and caregivers. It is his grace that teaches us how to train them.

The Nurture and Instruction of the Lord

In light of the number of books that have been written about parenting, the following statement may seem somewhat shocking: there are only two passages in the New Testament that give direct commands concerning it. Both are terse, to the point, and given without any profound explanation. They both contain a warning to fathers (and by implication to mothers who train children alongside them).

1. "Fathers, do not exasperate your children; instead, bring them up in the training and instruction of the Lord" (Eph. 6:4).

2. "Fathers, do not embitter your children, or they will become discouraged" (Col. 3:21).

Even though these two commands seem very basic and straightforward, perhaps we've failed to apprehend their true meaning. Perhaps the key to understanding discipline and instruction that is markedly Christian is assumed in the simple phrase most of us fail to take into account when we read these verses. The phrase? *Of the Lord*.[3]

Generally, whenever Paul uses the phrase "of the Lord," he is referring specifically to the Lord Jesus Christ.[4] Now, stop and think for a moment. Would the uniqueness of Christian parenting be clearer to you if this passage read, "Fathers, do not exasperate your children; instead, bring them up in the training and instruction of Jesus Christ"? Would that rewording spur you to think more specifically about Jesus, about his work? What would the training and instruction of Jesus look like? By suggesting this change in wording, we're not suggesting that we know better than the Holy Spirit how to craft Scripture. It's simply that the phrase "of the Lord" has become hackneyed Christianese to many of us. We hardly see it when we read it. It doesn't carry the same weight with us it carried with the original readers of Paul's letters. It was fresh and astounding and paradigm-shattering when they heard it. *Of the Lord?* they probably wondered. *What does that mean?* The Jews knew what the training and instruction of the rabbis looked like. The Greeks understood the discipline and instruction of their philosophers. But the training and instruction of the Lord? Of Jesus? What was that?

In the ancient Near East, Gentile (including Ephesian and Colossian) education included the training and instruction "of Greek philosophers." They learned logic, rhetoric, and speech, and were taught how to define and live a good life based on the teachings of men like Aristotle, Socrates, and Plato. The novel, radical message of grace turned everything they believed about parenting upside down. So, they would have wondered the same thing we do today. *"Of the Lord"? What does that mean?*

Neither the Jews nor the Greeks would have naturally employed training that was "of the Lord." It would have been a singularly peculiar phrase to them. Paul meant it to be so. Both those steeped in the law and those steeped in worldly philosophies would have had to think deeply about the implications of the good news as they sought to faithfully parent their children—just like we do.

In Ephesians, Paul employs two different words translated in the NIV as "training" and "instruction." One, *paideia*, means either to educate or train,[5] and the other, *nouthesia*, means "admonition, reprimand, instruct."[6] In other words, Paul is saying that the way Christian parents are to bring children up is by nurturing, educating, and training them in the truth of Jesus Christ and in the way he lived. Parents should daily tell the story and message about Jesus to their children and warn or rebuke them when they forget to live in light of what Jesus has already done. Every aspect of parenting should be tethered to the gospel message.

What does that look like today? Here are a few clarifying questions to help us get a better handle on what "of the Lord" parenting looks like:

- *How does Jesus becoming human change the way we speak to and treat our children?* God himself became a child in the person of Jesus. That one act of humility and identification as one of us shows us that he values children and teaches us to do the same. We are not to denigrate our children but speak to them and treat them with dignity.

- *What about the resurrection?* How does the truth of Christ's victory over sin and death make a difference when we guide our kids who are struggling with ongoing sin? Through his resurrection, Jesus brought justification to those who believe (Rom. 4:24–25), so if our children believe in him, they are justified. God looks at them not only as those who have never sinned but as those who have always obeyed. This truth makes a way for mercy and grace in our parenting and affirms our children in knowing that their standing with God doesn't change.

- *What does Christ's ascension and ongoing reign mean for our children in their everyday lives? For when they suffer loss or become discouraged?* "Because he always lives to intercede for them" (Heb. 7:25), and because Christ has suffered in every way, he can bring deep comfort to a child who feels lonely, anxious, or depressed.

Learning to apply the truths of Jesus's incarnation, sinless life, death in our place, bodily resurrection, ascension, reign, and return is what it means to raise our children in the nurture and instruction "of the Lord."

Manage, Nurture, and Love

Because the Bible is not primarily a manual on child-rearing but rather a proclamation of the good news, let's continue now by looking at four other passages that describe what "of the Lord" parenting would look like without giving actual direction on how to do it.

The first two of these passages describe faithful parenting as one of the qualifications for church leaders. In 1 Timothy 3:4–6, believers are qualified to be considered for eldership if they have "managed" their children, encouraging their children to obey. Likewise in verses 12–13, deacons are to have "managed" their households and children well.[7] Both elders and deacons (and their spouses) are called to oversee or manage the spiritual and natural affairs of the church. The home is the primary training ground for growth in management skills. There, in the home with their own flesh and blood, parents also learn how to appeal to those under their oversight to respond with respect and openness to the Lord's guidance.

Christian parents are to manage or oversee and admonish their children.[8] Christian children are to submit themselves to the management and direction of their parents. How do we help our children develop respect and openness to receive our instruction? A submissive heart is always the fruit of humility, an understanding of our helplessness and frailty. The humility that acquiesces to being led, managed, and trained flows out of an understanding of our own lostness and a growing understanding of and trust in God's wisdom for our lives. Only the good news of the gospel produces a true humility of heart that opens us to receive God's instruction.

The third and fourth descriptive passages focus more specifically on a mother's role. The first gives the qualifications of a widow deserving assistance from the church: a widow should be considered worthy of the church's support if she is "bringing up children" (5:10). This Greek phrase, also translated "nourished" or "nurtured," describes one of the primary traditional roles of a mother. Moms feed and nourish their children, both physically and spiritually. Generally speaking, women are nurturers. Typically, it is in both our physical design as those who can nourish babies from our own bodies and in our often natural posture and positioning as those who seek to meet the needs of those in our care whenever we can. The beautiful thing is that men are also nurturers, as Paul so pictures his ministry among the Thessalonians:

> We were not looking for praise from people, not from you or any-one else, even though as apostles of Christ we could have asserted our authority. Instead, we were like young children among you. Just as a nursing mother cares for her children, so we cared for you. Because we loved you so much, we were delighted to share with you not only the gospel of God but our lives as well. (1 Thess. 2:6–8; see also Isa. 66:13)

Our fourth passage, Titus 2:4, teaches us older women are to "train" younger women to love their children. We might wonder why mothers would need to be trained to love their children—until we recollect our own inability to love unconditionally. Younger women are to be encouraged to become nurturers in the same way God nurtures them.

In summary, then, the New Testament indirectly teaches fathers and mothers to manage their children—which means teaching them to obey rules meant for their and others' well-being; nurtur-ing them physically, spiritually, and emotionally; teaching them the ways of Jesus; and loving them dearly.

Words from the Old Testament

What about all those passages in the Old Testament that speak of parenting? Let's take a few moments to peruse these, too, as we seek to construct a methodology for parenting that is both biblical and "of the Lord."

Genesis 18:19 is the first passage in the Bible that describes a father's responsibilities. Speaking of Abraham, God states that his relationship with him began by God's choice, not Abraham's: "For I have chosen him." Then, in response to God's gracious choice, Abraham is to "direct his children and his household after him to keep the way of the LORD by doing what is right and just." Because of God's initiating grace in his life, Abraham is to direct his children to keep the way of the Lord.

On other occasions, the Lord sketches likely dialogue between parents and their children. The Lord assumes that, upon seeing his parents observe a feast day or recite the Law, a child will ask, "What does this mean?" In every instance, the answer is never primarily our obligation but rather God's grace. Here are some examples of proper answers and other instructions to be implemented in day-to-day conversation.

> And when your children ask you, "What does this ceremony mean to you?" then tell them, "It is the Passover sacrifice to the LORD, who passed over the houses of the Israelites in Egypt and spared our homes when he struck down the Egyptians." (Exod. 12:26–27)

> When your son asks you, "What does this mean?" say to him, "With a mighty hand the LORD brought us out of Egypt, out of the land of slavery." (13:14; see also Deut. 6:20–7:1; Josh. 4:21–23)

> Only be careful, and watch yourselves closely so that you do not forget the things your eyes have seen or let them fade from your heart as long as you live. Teach them to your children and to their children after them. (Deut. 4:9)

Because the Lord has loved us and made such great promises to us, we are to teach our children to love him with all their heart, all their soul, and all their might. When should we teach this to them? All the time.

> Love the LORD your God with all your heart and with all your soul and with all your strength. These commandments that I give you today are to be on your hearts. Impress them on your children. Talk about them when you sit at home and when you walk along the

road, when you lie down and when you get up. (Deut. 6:5–8; see also 11:19–21)

The psalmist longed to proclaim:

> Since my youth, God, you have taught me,
> and to this day I declare your marvelous deeds.
> Even when I am old and gray,
> do not forsake me, my God,
> till I declare your power to the next generation,
> your mighty acts to all who are to come.
> Your righteousness, God, reaches to the heavens,
> you who have done great things.
> Who is like you, God? (Ps. 71:17–19)

> We will not hide them from their descendants;
> we will tell the next generation
> the praiseworthy deeds of the LORD,
> his power, and the wonders he has done. (78:4)

What should be obvious by now is that even Old Testament parents didn't train and instruct their children solely in the law. They, too, were to give them grace. Why? Because they had been given grace, and only grace changes the heart. The law was always given *subsequent* to God's initiating mercy and always in the context of relationship with his children, *never* as a way to earn his blessing.

Breaking It Down

Now, what does everything we've learned look like in our everyday lives? Every situation will require different aspects of "of the Lord" parenting. Sometimes it will simply be about managing our children's behavior. Other times there will be more space and capacity to nurture and train them. And hopefully there will always be times we can correct and rehearse gospel promises to remind our children of the truth. So, let's break down these categories, and then work through a real-life example of what this could look like.

Managing

Ask yourself, *Is this a time to simply manage my children?* Sometimes children just need to be told what to do. "Go get in the car now." "Don't run in the street!" "Finish your homework and get ready for bed." "Sit quietly in church." Management includes training in the social, civic, and religious categories we talked about in chapter 1. A chart outlining everyone's daily responsibilities can help you manage the home, but again, care should be taken not to confuse compliance to management rules with true Christian righteousness. Management charts may help you run the home more smoothly, but they can also become your idol. Management is simply your effort to train outward behavior for the benefit of your children and those around your children. It is not meant to get to the heart, although a child's obedience to the outward rules *may* be evidences of faith. There is nothing wrong with just managing behavior. It is good and right and appropriate, but there are times you will be able to give your kids more than management.

Nurturing

Many times, children simply need hope that there is a God who loves them and has provided everything they need. Feed their souls with gospel truths of how Jesus has cared for them. One mom whose daughter was being rebellious laid out breakfast for her every morning with a little something special, like a flower or some blueberries. Her daughter later told her that the Lord used those little tokens to melt her heart. Even if your children refuse to open up to you or listen to you, you can still nurture their hearts.

Training

Children also need to learn how the gospel applies to the circumstance they're facing and what an appropriate response should be. There are times kids need a little help thinking through how to live in a loving and kind way. So, we take the time to train them. We don't assume they know the right thing to do and are just being disobedient or disrespectful. We help them make connections they are too young or inexperienced to see.

Correcting

Grace does not forbid us from correcting our children. But gospel correction reminds us to correct them in the context of what Jesus has already done for them and his great love for them. No one by nature always knows the right way to act. All of us have to be corrected and shown God's way to joy and freedom. Gospel correction is to be done in kindness and humility. We want to show our children how Jesus lived while on earth and the type of human he was, and then encourage them to follow him. We do this by reminding them of his great work for us and his love for his children.

Rehearsing Gospel Promises

Children need to be reminded of God's promises when they fail to believe he is as merciful and good as he says he is. He promises to love and care for them no matter their failures, and our children need these truths to be told to them again and again. Even though we have known God's promises, we often forget them, which is why it is good to be reminded and to remind our children of his covenant of love.

Here's an example of what "of the Lord" parenting might look like in a specific situation. Let's say your child makes the last out in a baseball game and throws a fit. What could you do? Let's break it down.

Category	Scripture Passages	Example
Managing Giving your children basic instructions for daily living.	1 Timothy 3:4–6, 12–13 Galatians 4:2–3	"Throwing your bat when you strike out is inappropriate behavior. You could hurt someone, and that's not okay."
Nurturing Feeding your children's souls with grace.	1 Timothy 5:10 1 Thessalonians 2:6–8 Psalm 78:4, 17–19	"I know you're sad that your team lost. I'm sure you feel disappointed, and it's okay to feel that way. I understand how you feel. Sometimes when I'm upset, I look up to the sky and see how high the heavens are above the earth, and I'm reminded that God loves me. Maybe later, we can look up at the sky together and be reminded of how much God loves you too, like he says in Ps. 103:11–12."
Training Teaching your children how the gospel applies to the circumstance they're facing and what an appropriate response should be.	Ephesians 6:4 Colossians 3:24	"I know that it's hard to set aside your sadness and congratulate the other team for a good game, but Jesus understands what it is like to love well when it is hard. He'll give you grace, and he'll help you do the kind thing."

Correcting Correcting your children in the context of what Jesus has already done for them and how they should respond in light of that.	Ephesians 6:4 Deuteronomy 4:9–14 Titus 2:11–14	"I know right now it seems like winning is all there is, but take some deep breaths and remember that your worth isn't in winning or losing. God loves you no matter what, and that's something that will never change. Don't forget what you have in the love of God. When you remember his love, winning will not seem as important."
Rehearsing Gospel Promises Reminding your children of God's promises when they fail to believe he is as merciful and good as he says he is.	John 3:16–18; 8:24 Acts 16:31 Romans 3:23–24; 4:22–25; 10:9–13	"What's most important is that you're beloved no matter what happens in a game. God promises he will never leave you nor forsake you. You can be confident that he will always hear you and give you grace and help when you need it. Rehearsing these promises brings so much joy and freedom. It helps you to remember what is most true about you. Winning or losing is temporary. Being loved is forever."

In this chapter, we've learned what the Bible has to say about how to raise our children. We've learned there are different facets of "of the Lord" parenting, and what is called for in one situation may not be what is best in the next. Here are some questions you can ask yourself to assess a situation and know how to move forward:

- Does this circumstance simply call for *management*?
- Now that the situation has calmed down, do I have an opportunity to *nurture* their souls with the gospel?
- Is this the time to *train* them in how to apply what Jesus has already done for them?
- Do I need to *correct* their attitudes or actions so that they are more in line with the good news?
- Should I *remind* them of God's promises, either of blessing for faith or punishment for unbelief?
- Finally, is this just a time for me to pray and ask the Lord to show me how the gospel applies to my own heart? Do I need clarity to understand why my child is struggling or resisting right now? Do I need clarity into my own heart's responses so that I am not sucked down into their unbelief, anger, or despair? What is it that bothers me about their attitude? Why?

These five categories—manage, nurture, train, correct, rehearse gospel promises—help us have some nuance in how we parent so it can more accurately reflect the phrase "of the Lord." But take heart: there is no command here to try to do every single one of them every time you speak to your children. Many times, and especially with younger children, all you're going to be able to do is manage them. I do want you to begin to pray that the Lord will help you remember to do more than that, but this isn't a new set of rules for you to follow. These are simply categories to help you as you parent in your everyday life.

"Think Over What I Say and Remember Jesus Christ"

Although the apostle Paul did not have a wife or children (as far as we know), he did have Timothy, his son in the faith. What follows is part of the fatherly advice he gives to him. As you read it, can you see how Paul nurtures, trains, and corrects Timothy in the Lord?

> You then, my son, be strong in the grace that is in Christ Jesus. . . . Join with me in suffering, like a good soldier of Christ Jesus. No one serving as a soldier gets entangled in civilian affairs, but rather tries to please his commanding officer. Similarly, anyone who competes as an athlete does not receive the victor's crown except by competing according to the rules. The hardworking farmer should be the first to receive a share of the crops. Reflect on what I am saying, for the Lord will give you insight into all this.
>
> Remember Jesus Christ, raised from the dead, descended from David. This is my gospel, for which I am suffering even to the point of being chained like a criminal. But God's word is not chained. (2 Tim. 2:1, 3–9)

Look again at that passage. Paul knows that only grace would strengthen his dear son. So before he speaks to Timothy about the work he needs to do, he reminds him of grace. Yes, he is to work hard, suffering like a soldier, an athlete, or a farmer, but the *gospel* is the context for all of it. Because of Christ, Timothy could do the hard work and join in Paul's suffering and be met with grace to persevere.

Paul's command to "bring them up in the training and instruction of the Lord" (Eph. 6:4) simply means this: parents are to think about and remember Jesus Christ and then train their children to understand how everything in their lives—all their joys and sorrows, all their trials and labors, all their doubts, sin, and shame—is to be understood and approached in the light of Jesus Christ, who died, rose from the dead, and is now working on their behalf to make them like him. This is the best news any child could hear.

Distinctly Christian parenting must be accomplished in the environment of the good news of Jesus Christ or it is not *Christian* parenting. It may work for a while, it may make our lives more manageable, and God may use it, but it is not "of the Lord."

As we close this chapter, let us nurture *ourselves* now with a soul-satisfying repast of grace from the psalms.

> Praise the LORD, my soul;
>> all my inmost being, praise his holy name.
>
> Praise the LORD, my soul,
>> and forget not all his benefits—
>
> who forgives all your sins
>> and heals all your diseases,
>
> who redeems your life from the pit
>> and crowns you with love and compassion,
>
> who satisfies your desires with good things
>> so that your youth is renewed like the eagle's.
>
> The LORD works righteousness
>> and justice for all the oppressed.
>
> He made known his ways to Moses,
>> his deeds to the people of Israel:
>
> The LORD is compassionate and gracious,
>> slow to anger, abounding in love.
>
> He will not always accuse,
>> nor will he harbor his anger forever;
>
> he does not treat us as our sins deserve
>> or repay us according to our iniquities.
>
> For as high as the heavens are above the earth,
>> so great is his love for those who fear him;
>
> as far as the east is from the west,
>> so far has he removed our transgressions from us.
>
> As a father has compassion on his children,
>> so the LORD has compassion on those who fear him;
>
> for he knows how we are formed,
>> he remembers that we are dust. (Ps. 103:1–14)

Remembering God's Grace

God is gracious and compassionate to you as you find your way through parenting. He's with you as he's with your children, loving and guiding you along the way. Take time to reflect on what you've learned in this chapter and answer these questions.

1) Understanding now that everything comes back to grace, how can you show yourself grace in your parenting?

2) How does your understanding of "of the Lord" parenting change the way you parent in everyday life?

3) Which of the five categories of gospel parenting (manage, nurture, train, correct, rehearse gospel promises) do you need some work in?

6

Wisdom Greater Than Solomon's

Praise his name, our God is glorious in wisdom. Kings came to learn of the wisdom of Solomon, but a greater than Solomon is here: Jesus Christ!

Edmund P. Clowney[1]

All their hopes had been trampled in the dust beneath the brutal heel of Rome's boot. For more than three years, they'd seen Jesus's miracles and heard his words. They became convinced. Surely he was the "one who is going to redeem Israel" (Luke 24:21). But then everything went terribly wrong. He was arrested, beaten, crucified. He was dead, and with him went all their hopes.

It was the day after the Sabbath, and life-as-usual had returned as it always did, draped now in shadows of hopelessness, futility, and confusion. *We thought we understood. We thought he was the One, the Messiah. How could we have been so mistaken?* And so Cleopas and his companion begin their sad trek together, up the road to Emmaus. They have no idea what awaits them on that road or how it would change everything they thought they knew.

While it was true Jesus had died and it had been days since he had been laid in Joseph's cold tomb, he is no longer held by death's grip. No, he is out walking on the road. His dear, grieving friends need something from him that would forever dispel their sadness and illumine their understanding. As they walk along the road, "Jesus himself" comes to walk beside them (v. 15). He asks them what they are discussing, and upon hearing their sorrow and confusion, he gradually opens their minds to understand the real meaning of the Old Testament Scriptures—*they are all about him* (John 5:39)! Here is how Luke describes their experience:

> And beginning with Moses and all the Prophets, he explained to them what was said in all the Scriptures concerning himself. . . . They asked each other, "Were not our hearts burning within us while he talked with us on the road and opened the Scriptures to us?" . . . He said to them, "This is what I told you while I was still with you: Everything must be fulfilled that is written about me in the Law of Moses, the Prophets and the Psalms." Then he opened their minds so they could understand the Scriptures. (Luke 24:27, 32, 44–45)

In essence, Jesus is teaching them that, "All truths come to their realization in relation to [him]."[2] When Jesus speaks of "the Law of Moses and the Prophets and the Psalms," he is referring to the entire Old Testament. Every passage of Scripture and every occurrence in all of creation has its fulfillment in Jesus Christ. "For in him all things were created . . . all things have been created through him and for him . . . that in everything he might have the supremacy," Paul writes (Col. 1:16, 18; see also Heb. 1:3–4). Jesus stands at the forefront of absolutely everything as supreme Lord over all!

So, why have we taken this jaunt up the Emmaus road to eavesdrop on a conversation when this is supposed to be a book about parenting? The reason is that we're about to wade into the wisdom of Proverbs, and I want you to understand how to read it in the light of the gospel of grace. Proverbs (and indeed, all of Scripture) is preeminently about Jesus's death, resurrection, and entrance into his glory (Luke 24:26). It is the Lord himself who teaches us to read the Proverbs asking this question: "Where is my Savior?"[3]

Seeing Jesus in Proverbs

For the most part, Proverbs was written by Solomon, the wisest man of his time (1 Kings 4:29–34), and although they are right and true words, not even Solomon was able to obey them himself or employ them in such a way that his own son wasn't foolish. Nevertheless, these proverbs were written to instill skill in the art of godly living in those who heed their counsel. Many are written as the words of a father to his son. Others are directed to parents as they seek to instill wisdom into their children.

If we approach Proverbs believing that the entire Bible "whispers his name,"[4] if we come with open eyes looking for our Savior, we'll easily identify him here as the Wise Son. The proverbs tell us how to live godly lives, but they also tell us about Jesus. For instance, the command, "My son, if sinners entice you, do not consent," was abundantly fulfilled in Jesus's resistance to Satan's temptations in the wilderness. Jesus is the Wise Son who always does what is pleasing to his Father (Isa. 52:13; John 8:29). And although the Bible is nearly silent about his childhood, we do have this one description: "Jesus increased in wisdom and in stature and in favor with God and man" (Luke 2:52 ESV). He was completely obedient because he was fully wise, and he was loved by his Father and his parents. Jesus even refers to himself as the personification of wisdom (Matt. 11:19), while Paul assures us that in him are hidden *all* the treasures of wisdom and knowledge (Col. 2:3). Jesus is the fulfillment of Proverbs.

But Jesus isn't merely the Wise Son who gladdens his Father's heart (Prov. 10:1; Matt. 3:17). He is also the Son who feels the rod of correction meant for fools. He is the one whom the Roman guards struck with their fists (Mark 14:65). Although completely blameless and wise, he received punishment (Prov. 26:3; Matt. 27:28–31). When the Holy Spirit opens our eyes to his presence, we see Jesus everywhere in the proverbs. Here is a man with wisdom greater and deeper than Solomon's (Matt. 12:42), treated like the fool who deserves punishment.

All of this is not to suggest that we ignore the plain teaching of Proverbs and instead simply look for Jesus. No, the plain words of Proverbs are for our good, and we will grow in wisdom if we respond to them in faith and humility. However, if we neglect to see Jesus in them too, we will wrongly assume we will automatically be able to accomplish something not even Solomon could do: produce wise children. In addition, because the proverbs are so clear-cut and seem like promises, we'll mistakenly believe our performance will guarantee success.

Discipline and the Gospel

Every parent must come to his or her own conclusion about the method of discipline to be administered. Although Proverbs enjoins appropriate and loving use of physical force, what it calls "the rod," or spanking (13:24; 22:15; 29:15), the New Testament is silent on the methods parents should employ. While it is true that Hebrews 12 does talk about discipline being painful, that doesn't necessitate the use of physical force. Sometimes taking away a device or restricting interaction with friends qualifies as painful discipline. Recent studies have shown the brain is impacted in harmful ways when children are exposed to physical pain as a form of discipline.[5] While not all people agree with these findings, parents should be aware of them and then make their own decisions.

Although many sincere Christians disagree, correction or discipline must come in the context of the Wise Son who took punishment meant for fools. Here's how a conversation before or after a time of discipline might sound for our beloved second child, David, from chapter 4.

> David, I'm grieved that you decided to disobey me when I clearly told you that it was time to put away your toys and get ready for supper. Because you blatantly defied my request and continued to play, even though you knew we were waiting for you, now I have to discipline you. I'm doing this because, as your parent, my responsibility to love and care for you means that I need to teach you to listen and obey. I know we're both sad that discipline can be painful, but it's a reminder for us both that Jesus willingly took the discipline—the punishment—we were supposed to receive from God because he loved us.
>
> If you believe he loves you and received punishment for you, then this kind of punishment will help remind you to live wisely, and the pain of it will soon be gone. But if you don't believe in his great goodness and don't choose to live wisely moving forward, then the punishment you receive today will be just the beginning of an unnecessarily difficult life of pain. I'm praying the Holy Spirit changes your heart to be truly sorry for disobeying me, and if you ask for forgiveness, God will forgive you and so will I. I hope this discipline teaches you that pain always follows disobedience and also that I need to discipline you because I love you.

Can you see how the gospel makes a difference in the tone and content of such times of discipline? This isn't a script to be memorized but rather a model to encourage you to point to Jesus Christ even while lovingly disciplining your children. As you pray for wisdom and ask the Holy Spirit to remind you of the gospel, you'll find that your heart is softened and encouraged too, helping you discover the sweetness of the gospel when you have to go through discipline yourself.

The good news teaches us that the record of the Wise Son has been given to believing children, and that doesn't change even during times of discipline. Although some children compound their sin during discipline by being stubbornly angry or sullen, they can be reassured that because Jesus suffered through his time of punishment perfectly, without sinning, his record is their record too if they believe in him. Times of correction are to be times of gospel witness, reminding children that Jesus knows what it is to be punished, that he bore all the punishment upon himself even though he didn't deserve it, and that they are forgiven and restored in relationship to God because of him.

Is This Purposeful Disobedience or Immaturity?

Of course, before we discipline, we need to be sure our children understand what we're asking of them and are capable of obeying. Perhaps their disobedience is a matter of immaturity. Or perhaps it is a matter of neurodivergence. The more research is done on the brain, the more our understanding grows when it comes to neurodivergent children. There are children who are mentally unable to function in a way we would consider "typical." This inability is no fault of their own, and a wise parent will be on the lookout for this, not always assuming the child has the ability to do what is being asked.

Paul writes, "When I was a child, I talked like a child, I thought like a child, I reasoned like a child. When I became a man, I put the ways of childhood behind me" (1 Cor. 13:11). Our children are childish because they are not adults. They speak, think, and reason like children because they are children. Their childish ways may be sinful or they may be evidence of weakness or inability in thinking ahead, weighing consequences, managing their time, remembering what they were supposed to be doing, or saying the right thing. There is a difference between childishness and foolishness. One is the result of normal immaturity. The other is the result of sin. While we want to be diligent to train them so they mature into responsible adults and give up their childish ways, careful thought needs to be given as to whether their actions are the fruit of willful defiance or simple childishness. Does this disobedience call for correction, or is this time to be sure the child is capable of obedience?

When a two-year-old continues to try to touch something he shouldn't touch (for whatever reason) his parent should move his hand and tell him "no." Perhaps he could be given something else to play with instead. Toddlers don't need explanations. They simply need to be kept from danger and taught to obey Mom and Dad's voice. This outward management does not transform their hearts or make them more receptive to grace. We don't have that kind of power over their hearts. It simply teaches them how to obey outwardly.

If our little toddler continues to try to grab the object or falls down on the ground crying because he is being denied, the level of correction should be stepped up. He is not old enough to understand all the ramifications of his disobedience. He is still thinking and reasoning like a child. He simply has to be taught to obey those in authority over him who care about him. He should then be hugged and sent along to play again. This is the kind of training that falls into the management category we talked about in chapter 5. If we manage our children in this way while they are very young, frequently we'll find that the necessity for correction lessens as they mature. Some children are very compliant and learn quickly to move their hand in another direction when Mommy says no. Others are more resistant and need the same lesson over and over again.

Depending on the maturity of the child, time spent in gospel instruction (nurturing, training, correcting, rehearsing gospel promises) should begin to increase even as the need for actual correction decreases. The more a child understands and believes the gospel, the more their parent is able to reason with them. Personally, I (Jessica) have seen the Holy Spirit transform my son's proud heart more deeply than anything I have done. Our goal is always to get to the point where we are talking with our kids about the truth of the gospel more and more, believing their training will be brought about by the conviction of the Holy Spirit instead of by what we do. We can learn that our children are moving toward maturity when it doesn't take our correction to start them in the direction of repentance.

Sometimes we may feel like we are in a season when we are doing nothing but disciplining, and that when we share the gospel with our children they act as though they've never heard it before. Sometimes it is months before we see any fruit from all our effort. When it's wintertime in their souls, this is when we need to continue to obey in faith, believe the Lord will use our efforts to bless our children, recite the gospel over and over to ourselves, and wait and pray for the life-giving work of the Holy Spirit.[6]

Relationships in the Family

Some parents insist children immediately ask for forgiveness for their offenses, sometimes in order for the correction to cease. Although Elyse and I know parents long for immediate reconciliation and repentance, we disagree with this practice. It is never advisable to tempt children to lie. Certainly, children should be taught that pain is a consequence for disobedience and that their disobedience affects others, not just themselves. They should be encouraged to ask God and others (including their parents) for forgiveness, but only if they are genuinely sorry.

When parents encourage children to ask for forgiveness when their hearts haven't been moved by Holy Spirit's conviction, we are training them to be hypocritical and false. And we are inadvertently teaching them that false professions of sorrow will satisfy

God. God is never pleased with outward proclamations of devotion when the heart is far from him (Isa. 29:13; Matt. 15:7–9); in fact, he hates them. However, we can never know with absolute certainty whether or not their proclamations of repentance are true because only God knows the heart (Jer. 17:9–10). Assuming we can see into the heart is a sign of our pride and is dangerous for our children.

Rather than insisting on an immediate show of repentance, we should give children time to respond to the prompting of the Holy Spirit. Assure them you are praying for them. Ask them to wait for a while and pray that they will have grace to understand and change. And then leave them in the hands of the Holy Spirit. When you do, you'll be amazed at how quickly many of them will come around and willingly ask for forgiveness. But even if they don't, you can and should continue to lavish them with your love, confessing your own unbelief, disobedience, and faith in God's promise to continue to love you even though you don't see or confess even one tenth of your own sin. We don't have to sever our relationship with unrepentant children because their relationship with us is not based on their merit but rather on the ties of family love. All of our relationships are based on and must reflect our relationship with the Lord. Our sin does grieve him, but if we are in Christ, our sin can never separate us from him.

> "God does not slack his promises because of our sins," says Paul in essence, "or hasten them because of our righteousness and merits. He pays no attention to either."[7]

I am not telling you to ignore bad behavior, nor am I saying that sinful behavior should not be corrected. What I am saying is that we should not teach our children that sinful behavior alters their relationship with us. If our parenting is modeled on the gospel, then their sin, hardness, and unbelief will grieve us, but we will seek to discipline and correct it. We will pray for them about it, and we will continue to love and welcome them in spite of it. But we will not demand a *show* of repentance before we welcome them back into relationship. It is better for our children to learn to live in unresolved conflict than to force them into a fake peace.

Remembering that genuine love for God and others will *only* grow in the environment of his initiating love for us will help us when we are fearful and are tempted to demand some show of repentance from our children to ease our concerns. As they struggle with true repentance and godly sorrow, we can calm our anxious hearts by remembering these precious words from Martin Luther:

> But because we have only the first fruits of the Spirit, and the remnants of sin still remain in us, we do not obey the law perfectly. But this imperfection is not imputed to us who are in Christ [who] has blessed us. . . . *We are nourished and tenderly cherished for Christ's sake, in the lap of God's longsuffering.*[8]

Beautiful, comforting words! Nourish and tenderly cherish your children in the lap of your longsuffering and entrust them into the hands of a faithful Savior who alone has the ability to transform their hearts.

Although we all long for some assurance that our children are responding or that we are doing the right thing, we don't need to do God's work for him. He was able to save your soul and raise you up in understanding his love and grace. He's able to save their souls and raise them up too.

> Grace frees us from having to earn God's acceptance by meeting others' expectations, and it also frees us from the unholy pride and prejudice of determining others' acceptance by God on the basis of our own wisdom.[9]

You Are My Beloved Child, Now Live into It

Seminary president Bryan Chapell reflects on the shift in his own parenting as he began to be touched by the truths of grace:

> I used to say to my son, "Colin, because of what you did you are a bad boy." I would characterize him by his actions. But then I recognized that this is not the way that God treats me. The grace that identifies me as God's child is not based on my actions. He characterizes me based on my relationship with him not on the basis of what I have done. My union with Christ (the indicative of who I am) precedes and motivates my obedience (the imperative). Thus, to treat our children as God treats us, my wife and I put ourselves under the discipline of saying to our son, "Colin, don't do that, because you are my child." In essence, we urged our son, "Be what you are, our beloved," rather than, "Do, so you will be beloved."[10]

This is the pattern for training in obedience that we find throughout the Scriptures. For example, in 1 Thessalonians 5, Paul does this very thing. He tells the Thessalonian believers who they are: "children of light, children of the day," and he tells them who they are not: children "of the night or of the darkness" (v. 5 ESV). After reminding them of their identity, he tells them how to live: soberly, with faith, love, and hope. Then, *again*, he reminds them of their status before the Father: they are not "[appointed] to suffer wrath but to receive salvation through our Lord Jesus Christ" (v. 9). Then, *again*, he reminds them of the good news: Jesus Christ is the one who "died for us so that . . . we may live together with him" (v. 10), *again* reminding them of relationship. And finally, in verse 11 he tells them to use these words to encourage and build up one another.[11] If you want your parenting to be based on the Bible, *this must be the ruling model for it*. Remind your children who they are because of how God sees them and remind them of your love and welcome. Then remind them of

God's gracious offer of salvation through faith in Jesus Christ. Only then can you teach obedience.

The writer of Proverbs directs his advice toward "his son" at least twenty-two times.[12] He pleads with his son to take the training he is giving him to heart: "Hear, my son, your father's instruction, and forsake not your mother's teaching" (Prov. 1:8 ESV). He appeals to him to live wisely and thereby comfort his father's heart and make it glad: "My son, if your heart is wise, then my heart will be glad indeed; my inmost being will rejoice when your lips speak what is right" (23:15–16). This is no detached training from a drill sergeant. This father has anchored his gladness in his son's wisdom, much like the apostle John does in 3 John 4: "I have no greater joy than to hear my children are walking in the truth." This father goes so far as to entreat his son to give him his heart and invites him into his life, to learn by observing his ways (Prov. 23:26). This is training in a loving, committed relationship.

These commands are given in the context of a son's relationship with both his father and mother.[13] Both parents train their child in wise living. Solomon is appealing to his son to remember the love he has received and to react in kind. He says, in so many words, "You are my dearly beloved son; please remember who you already are and live like it."

Donkeys, Carrots, and Sticks

Everyone struggles with obedience, no matter how old they are. Little children who want to touch what Daddy has said not to. Older children who refuse to share their toys even though they know they should. Teens who sneak their cell phones out to text their friends when they should be studying. Adults who know they are commanded to love their neighbors but gossip about them anyway. No matter what our age or our maturity in Christ, everyone has a problem with sin—even the apostle Paul, who confesses,

"For I do not do the good I want to do, but the evil I do not want to do—this I keep on doing" (Rom. 7:19).

Every parent has a theory of training and motivation, an underlying belief of how to get kids to do what they want, whether it's clearly stated or not. During the 1800s, one theory based on promises of reward and threats of punishment was developed. Basically, this theory proposed there were two ways to get a donkey to move a cart. First, you could dangle a carrot in front of the donkey, fooling the donkey into thinking that if it pulled the cart far enough, it would get to eat the carrot. Second, you could prod the donkey along the road by hitting it with a stick. If the donkey is motivated by the ultimate reward of a carrot, it will not need to feel the stick. But if it's not really all that interested in carrots, then the stick will be employed. Either way, through reward or through punishment, the donkey's owner gets the desired result.

I can remember learning this motivational paradigm when I (Elyse) taught in a Christian school in the 1970s and early '80s. I remember a cartoon of a silly looking donkey moseying down the road with a carrot dangling in front of its dim eyes and a farmer seated on the cart behind it with a whip. It seemed logical to me. Motivate the kids with a reward or motivate them with punishment. Either way was fine, as long as they got down the road.

I'm sorry to say that I carried this philosophy over into my home with my own children. When they behaved, they got to put beans in a jar to earn a trip to the ice-cream shop. When they failed to behave, beans were removed. If one child disobeyed, the others suffered for it and would pressure the rebel to fall into line. I really believed the carrots and sticks were working well with my little donkeys. But there were several significant problems: my children weren't donkeys; they were image-bearers of God. Also, I wasn't ultimately in charge; he was. And, of course, we had completely overlooked the gospel.

How would the gospel transform this carrot-stick motivational paradigm? Quite simply by turning the entire model on its head.

Because both parents and children obstinately refuse to pull the cart of God's glory down the road, the Father has broken the stick of punishment on his obedient Son's back. Rather than trying to entice us by incessantly dangling an unattainable carrot of perfect welcome and forgiveness in front of our faces, God the Father freely feeds the carrot to us, his enemies. He simply moves outside all of our categories for reward and punishment, for human motivation, and gives us all the reward as he takes upon himself all the punishment. He lavishes grace upon grace on us and bears in his own person all the wrath we deserve. Then he tells us, in light of all he's done, "Obey."

Yes, we do have promises of rewards in heaven, but these are not earned by us through our merit. Yes, there are promises of punishment, but not for those who believe and put their faith in Christ. All our punishment has been borne by him. The carrot is ours. The stick is his to bear. Manage your kids with beans in a jar if you must, but be sure to tell them that this isn't the gospel. And perhaps, once in a while, just fill the jar up with beans and take everyone out for ice cream—and when your son asks you, "Daddy, why are we getting ice cream? How did the jar get to be full?" you'll know what to say, won't you?

Deeper Wisdom from the Proverbs

As we close our time thinking about the proverbs, here are two more verses to help you wrestle through what we've talked about. The first is Proverbs 16:7: "When the LORD takes pleasure in anyone's way, he causes their enemies to make peace with them." How would you explain this verse to your children? You might say something like, "When you live in the light of the wisdom God gives, you'll usually find you can live in peace with people— even your enemies." But it's best if, after you say that, you add, "Although that's true, we also know that Jesus's ways pleased the Lord, but his enemies killed him. And that's not all. By his sacrifice, he made his enemies (you and me) his friends—it changed our relationship with him! We're at peace with him right now because he bore all the wrath we deserved. Isn't that good news?"

Here's one final proverb: "Acquitting the guilty and condemning the innocent—the LORD detests them both" (17:15). If we fail to see the Wise Son who received blows meant for a fool, we'll miss the depth of this wisdom. Of course, having righteous judgment pleases God. But Jesus is the one who justifies the wicked. The Father is the one who condemned the perfectly righteous one. Why? So that we would no longer be considered wicked, would move out of our tit-for-tat world and into the grace of the gospel of Jesus Christ, and would be overwhelmed by his wisdom and grace and bathe our dear children in joy and freedom every day.

Remembering God's Grace

Learning to parent with grace and wisdom takes time and help from the Holy Spirit. You will make mistakes. Your kids won't listen. There will be tears from all parties involved. But there is always room for repairing the relationship, for grace to cover everyone, for mercies to be new again the next morning and even the next moment. Now, in order to soak in the learning from this chapter, take time to reflect on these questions.

1) What is the difference between sin and immaturity? How have you expected too much maturity from your children or overlooked sin in their behavior?

2) If you ever treat your children differently or hold them at arm's length after you have disciplined them, how can you welcome them back into loving relationship freely?

_____

_____

3) What truth is God telling you about yourself as a parent? How can the gospel encourage you where you're at?

_____

_____

7

The One Good Story to Guide All Parenting Decisions

The Son of Man has come eating and drinking, and you say, "Look, a glutton and a drunkard, a friend of tax collectors and sinners!"

Luke 7:34 CSB

Imagine this: the great King sends his beloved Son to sojourn in the land he owns. Because the people are under the influence of a wicked impostor, rather than loving this stranger, the natives of the land do him wrong. They do not love him; they do not remember that they were once strangers who had been loved. They forget all the great King's commands, and instead they kill his Son. Yet the King, in his great love for the people, blesses and forgives them. Then, miraculously, he raises his beloved Son from the dead to ensure that the people of the land are cared for forever. This is the One Good Story.

Wisdom through the Gospel

Every parent knows what it is like to have to make decisions about their children's clothing, hairstyles, entertainment, and relationships. If there were a place where a tidy list of dos and don'ts would fit nicely, this would be it. It would be very easy for Jessica and me to say, "Keep your children from every outside influence," and simply leave the matter there. But you know us well enough by now to know that isn't what we're going to do. We refuse to give you more law to impose on your children because the law doesn't breed obedience and love. It only produces pride and despair—for you, for them—and it won't ever produce the joy that is to be our strength.

We're going to help you learn how to approach every decision with the One Good Story, the gospel story, in mind (see the appendix). We know this won't be as easy as having a list to go by, at least not at first, but it will encourage dependence on the Holy Spirit and nourish the entire family's souls. So, as an introduction to get your thinking going in the right direction, here are a few questions to ask yourself when you're faced with a decision that isn't clearly spelled out in Scripture.

- What does the gospel teach me about this choice or this situation?
- Where do I see the great King in this? What is he showing me about himself?
- What does the life of the beloved Son teach me about how to work through this?
- Is this a trick of the wicked impostor? Is this a work of human brokenness or perhaps even evil?

- What am I believing and/or teaching when I forbid/allow this? Is this something I need to simply let go of and see where it goes?

- Is my allowance of this choice a function of love for God or love of the world, or is it something else?

- How am I loving my neighbor as I love God and myself in this situation, and how are my decisions and actions reflective of Christlikeness? Am I remembering the Great Commandment to love my neighbors and seeking to fulfill the Great Commission to share the gospel with them as part of our relationship?

- How am I being wise in determining what's good or bad in what we value as a family or for our children? What is the Holy Spirit teaching me about what to uphold as good and right, and what is simply another way to impose more laws?

Do those questions seem too complex? If so, know that you don't need to remember every single one of them all the time. This is simply a way for you to reframe your thinking; it's a way to gain wisdom as you do your best to immerse yourself and your children in the good news. If you try to remember that you have a loving heavenly Father, the great King, who sent his beloved Son into the world to undo all the sadness and deception the wicked impostor has brought, you'll be headed in the right direction. If you remember what Jesus has already done for you, your family, and your unbelieving neighbors, and if you ask the Holy Spirit for help, you'll find these kinds of decisions becoming easier to make. But even if you don't remember to ask yourself these questions, even if you make a decision without thinking about the gospel, the Lord is faithful to use everything in your life for your good and his glory.

So Many Different Opinions

Jessica and I are very well aware that there is a great diversity of opinion among sincere believers surrounding decisions that have no clear answers and require wisdom. It's in these situations that our attachment to law-making and control show up most glaringly. Because of their loving desire to protect their children from the evil in the world, some parents live more like reclusive monks than first-century Christians, who were famous for their love for and service within their cities—cities that were frequently much more overtly wicked than those typically found in modern-day America. For instance, goddess worship, temple prostitution, superstition, sorcery, infanticide, and child slavery were commonplace in the two cities that Paul writes his parental directives to, Ephesus and Colossae. In the midst of all this evil and degradation, Paul does not command parents to remove their children from these cities and take flight to the suburbs to raise them in an environment more conducive to holiness. Sure, there were reclusive sects in the ancient Near East, but they were insignificant, definitely not those who turned the world upside down. How could they have been? They shunned interaction with the world and with the people who live within it.

On the other hand, some parents are so foolishly cavalier about what they expose their children to that they acquaint them with every sort of base influence without taking the time to discern their child's inability to understand or resist the deceptions within them. They pay no attention to ratings on video games, music, movies, or social media platforms, fearing that their children will resent their interference if they restrict them from what all their friends enjoy. Surely the Lord who invited little children up onto his lap for a hug would not want them thrown into the cesspools those mediums often can offer.

Such issues with many opinions are commonly called "wisdom issues," so let's try to discern wisdom by examining the Scriptures through the lens of the One Good Story.

Come Out from Among Them

It is interesting to note that parents are nowhere in the Bible specifically commanded to keep their children secluded from the people of the world. The verses that come closest to doing so are those concerning the marriage of Israelites to unbelieving Gentiles, such as,

> Make no treaty with them, and show them no mercy. Do not intermarry with them. Do not give your daughters to their sons or take their daughters for your sons, for they will turn your children away from following me to serve other gods, and the Lord's anger will burn against you and will quickly destroy you. (Deut. 7:2–4)[1]

Under the old covenant, this law was so significant that the exiles who returned to Israel after the Babylonian captivity were commanded to divorce their pagan wives. Because fathers usually arranged marriages for their children (both sons and daughters), this command forbade them from doing so, with some gloriously gracious exceptions.[2] This law was primarily focused on the national purity of Israel, but there was also a spiritual component involved. The Lord wanted his children's hearts to be free from the worship of the idols of the nations that surrounded them, and living intimately with an idolater would create unnecessary temptation and discord.

This law against entanglement with unbelieving neighbors is recast in an interesting way in the New Testament. Whereas the Old Testament saints were forbidden from marrying Gentiles, and returning exiles were even commanded to divorce them, married Corinthians who became believers were not commanded to divorce their unbelieving partners. Paul writes in 1 Corinthians 7 that the believing partner's influence in the home set the unbeliever apart from "other unbelievers and from the evil of the world."[3] Because of their intimate relationship, the believer was in a position to bless the unbeliever through the daily demonstration of their faith.[4]

In another well-known passage, 2 Corinthians 6:14–16, Paul warns believers against being "yoked" with unbelievers. This passage has broad implications; Paul is not speaking specifically about marriage here, or even about avoiding worldly influences. Rather he is labeling those who have resisted him from *within* the congregation—those who say they are believers but do not submit to his apostolic authority—as the "unbelievers" with whom true believers should not identify.[5] More broadly, Christian children and their parents are clearly warned against being "yoked together" or allied with those who oppose Christ's authority in the church in such a way that the "unbeliever" has the power to strongly direct, control, or influence the believer. Paul is referring to people *within* the local church who are masquerading as believers, not unbelievers outside the church. Associations with unbelievers outside the church are not to be shunned (1 Cor. 5:10) but rather undertaken with wisdom.

This interpretation of these two passages from 1 and 2 Corinthians harmonizes beautifully with the story of the beloved Son, doesn't it? When we consider his mission, his total immersion within our sinful world, we can see how he does not call us away from unbelievers but rather calls us to follow him into relationship with them. He sees our presence in their lives as a way to show them the goodness of the gospel for his glory. This is the principle clearly demonstrated by Jesus's blatant disregard of the clean/unclean distinctions when touching lepers (Matt. 8:3) and the dead (Mark 5:41; Luke 7:14). To the Lord Jesus, a Samaritan woman (John 4:9) is not unclean. She is a thirsty soul who needs a drink of his life-transforming living water. He hangs around with sinners and tax collectors (Matt. 9:10–11; 11:19; Luke 15:1) and by doing so infuriates those who pride themselves on their separation from the world and their punctilious law-keeping. His holiness rubs off on those considered outsiders rather than the other way around. His presence in our sinful world does not pollute his holiness. Rather he identifies with us and dwells among us (John 1:1) for the very purpose of making us holy.

This message of integration rocked the early Jewish church to its core. Peter himself needed a shocking visit from God to overcome his prejudice against those outside the family of faith, even though he spent years watching Jesus interact with Gentiles and sinners. Here is Peter's testimony about his change of heart:

> You are well aware that it is against our law for a Jew to associate with or visit a Gentile. But God has shown me that I should not call anyone impure or unclean. (Acts 10:28; see also Rom. 14:14; 1 Cor. 5:9–10)

It's very important for our study to notice that the "unlawful" associations Peter is referring to here are not restrictions imposed by the Lord. No, they are mere Jewish tradition, a legalistic fencing off of the nation from those around her to preserve her "purity." In an effort to be "super holy," the Pharisees had expanded God's prohibitions about mixture in marriage and worship to forbid any association with unbelievers at all. Peter was taught not to associate with or visit anyone who was not Jewish. *This was never God's plan for his people.* Peter really struggled against his own conscience in embracing this truth later in Antioch (Gal. 2:11–14). Paul violently opposed his misguided exclusivity in the strongest way, saying that he was "not acting in line with the truth of the gospel" (v. 14).

Peter had to learn that God had never commanded his people to disassociate themselves with unbelievers. Rather, they had been ordained to be a blessing to unbelievers. The commissioning of the early church in Acts 1:8 includes taking this good news to every part of the earth, outside of our little family circle and especially into our neighborhoods. Let's face it: it's impossible to be a witness to unbelieving neighbors if we shun them because we're afraid they will pollute our families.

Here are a few questions to ask yourself about your children and the friends they make as you construct a framework for relating to those outside of your family circle:

- Have my children's friends been taught about appropriate behavior, or have they been taught but are choosing to ignore it?
- Do these friends hold some sort of strong influence over my children that I should protect them from?
- Are my children able to articulate proper boundaries?
- Do my children love Jesus and want to follow him? Do these friends encourage them in this?
- Is this a safe time to allow my children the possibility of making a mistake in their choices and possibly experiencing negative consequences?

Bad Company? Or Wise?

Another passage that is often used to bolster arguments for a more secluded family life is from 1 Corinthians: "Do not be misled: 'Bad company corrupts good character'" (15:33). Paul's point in using this quotation is summed up well in Eugene Peterson's paraphrase of Scripture: "Don't let yourselves be poisoned by this anti-resurrection loose talk. 'Bad company ruins good manners'" (MSG). Paul is warning about the dangers of association with those within the church who deny the resurrection. He's not making a comment about whether children of believers should associate with unbelieving children.

However, it is obvious that we do become like those we most closely associate with. Proverbs 13:20 teaches us, "Walk with the wise and become wise, for a companion of fools suffers harm." Let's say your child wants to hang out at a new friend's house after school, and you aren't sure you should let them. You haven't gotten to know this friend or their parents yet, so you're hesitant. At the same time, you want to encourage your child to discern for themselves what kinds of friends they should be making and how to be wise and stay safe in an unfamiliar situation. Here are some questions you might consider asking yourself:

- Is my child old enough and mature enough to make wise and safe decisions for themselves? Have they shown me this by the choices they've made before?
- Do I have a trusting relationship with my child where they know that even if they make mistakes they'll be loved and forgiven?
- Are they familiar with the life of Jesus and understand what loving God and loving others looks like in their friendships?
- Is this a time for managing, nurturing, training, correcting, or rehearsing gospel promises?
- And more practically, can this hangout happen at our house instead of theirs while I get to know the friend and the friend's family?
- What compromise can I make with my child that reflects parenting with grace?

We want our children to learn how to determine who is wise company and how to make wise choices when it comes to what they do with their friends, what they watch, how they carry themselves, and where they find their identity, belonging, and worth. We want our children to know and believe the One Good Story and have that be their guiding compass. In everything they surround themselves with and immerse themselves in, we want them to be able to recognize the great themes of the gospel: sacrificial love, the laying down of our lives for our enemies, miraculous resurrection, extravagant kindness, and sovereign reign. We want them to identify forgiveness, justice, redemption, and the fight against evil, whether that comes from watching a movie, observing friendship dynamics, or taking in the news. Saturating our children in the One Good Story and teaching them how to live it out will help them discern both truth and error as it comes to them from all areas of their lives.

Why Let Them See Anything at All?

Media and access to it has changed so much over the years, and many of us are concerned about how it's affecting our children. Why allow our children to be familiar with any modern media at all? Why not just limit what they listen to, watch, and read to what we listened to, watched, and read when we were young or to what is considered "Christian"? The gospel gives us three reasons.

First, our children will eventually grow up and become self-governing individuals. This is a good and natural part of life. Our hope is that if we have taught them how to seek and find the One Good Story and judge every other story by it, they'll be better equipped to answer the wicked impostor's lies when they hear them.

Second, the gospel tells us that evil does not have its origin solely outside us. Jesus himself corrected the Pharisees' misconception about what defiles a person when he said, "What comes *out* of a person is what defiles them" (Mark 7:20). Our propensity for evil is basic and insidious to our nature. We don't need anyone to teach us how to sin, and until we are fully redeemed when Christ returns, we remain prone to sin. It comes to us from our own human, sinful nature, and even though we might try to protect ourselves from it, as M. Night Shyamalan's 2004 movie, *The Village*, demonstrates, we just can't keep it out. Wherever we are, evil is there—not just the potential for evil, but real evil. Without Christ, what is already in our hearts is what defiles us, not what comes to us from media. While we should teach our kids how to navigate media wisely, we should also teach them to be aware of their sin. This is where the One Good Story comes in. Recognizing their sin will show them their need for a Savior and Helper, which points them to Jesus.

Finally, the gospel teaches us that God has called us to minister to this media-saturated culture. Whether we like it or not, music, TV, movies, and social media is the language our society speaks, and those mediums inform and shape our culture's philosophies and desires. We are different, however, not because we don't participate or enjoy the media but because we know the story of all stories. We have a God whose presence satisfies us more. We find joy and hope and connection in Christ that these mediums cannot provide, and this is what we want everyone to know about.

Of course, we're not saying that every movie or media form is suitable or beneficial for our children. Some things are, and some TV shows and movies are so iconic that at least a familiarity with them is necessary to build bridges to their peers and friends. We don't want to be so disconnected with our current culture that we cannot find common ground with those outside our family or faith. We want to be able to hang out and become friends so that, in relationship with them, we can show them the love of God. However, if you're looking for some wisdom on media exposure, here are some questions you can ask yourself:

- Does this media have any redeeming value to it? In other words, is there any way I can use it to illustrate the One Good Story?

- Are my children unduly influenced by it? Do they mimic inappropriate words or phrases after spending time interacting with it? Do they find themselves addicted to keep watching or keep scrolling?

- Are my children able to articulate what is lacking in this media? Do they see the ways it is contrary to the gospel and the ways it tells the One Good Story?

- What is my children's attitude when denied this media? Has it become an idol in their hearts, a god that promises them happiness?

- Is there any way I can demonstrate a willingness to compromise with my children over this media? For instance, instead of saying no to an entire album, can I find a couple of songs on it that would be acceptable?

- Am I being ruled by fear of what might happen if my children watch or listen to this media? Or am I able to think clearly and wisely about the influence the entertainment may or may not have over my kids?

Remember They Are Still Children

Children are children because they are still thinking and reasoning in childish ways. They do not have the maturity to filter out words and images that overwhelm them, so we have the responsibility to protect their childlikeness. We need to be wise for them, which means we sometimes make decisions on their behalf and other times determine what they're exposed to or what they can handle.

First, let's discuss how we should protect what they take in. We know from Scripture that words can enter the heart or inner person of children and adults (Ps. 119:11; Jer. 15:16). Because of this, little children should be sheltered from images that are frightening; they don't understand there is a way to make an image look real on the movie screen that is not actually real. In their childishness, they simply believe their eyes. So when they see something that is overwhelmingly scary, they'll take that image with them.

Children should also be protected from images that portray boys and girls or men and women acting in ways that are not age appropriate. Little children do not need to watch any illicit or prolonged sexual content because they are still reasoning like children. They do not understand the nuances of what's right or wrong or what's healthy or not in relationships. What they witness from their parents' healthy, committed, and loving relationship is, of course, different.

Second, kids should be protected from thinking their worth is measured by how they look, by how they dress, or by who likes them or approves of them. In Christian circles, we often elevate the idea of modesty as the standard for how our children should dress and carry themselves. *Modesty* is commonly defined in an overly simplistic way as "Don't wear this, don't do that." But true modesty is much deeper than this. To discover gospel truth here, we've got to define modesty in light of the One Good Story.

Here's a passage that describes the modesty of the beloved Son:

> Have this mind among yourselves, which is yours in Christ Jesus, who, though he was in the form of God, did not count equality with God a thing to be grasped, but made himself nothing, taking the form of a servant, being born in the likeness of men. And being found in human form, he humbled himself by becoming obedient to the point of death, even death on a cross. (Phil. 2:5–8 ESV)

The modesty we see in Jesus's life is a refusal to show off or insist that everyone give him his due. He didn't proclaim his greatness in the streets (Matt. 12:19) or show off in front of his enemy (4:1–11). Although he could have called down legions of angels or obliterated all his detractors and the ever-so-slow disciples, he restrained himself. He didn't need their approval or praise. He had nothing to prove, and he lived humbly and confidently in who he was.

Further, when it comes to modesty with regard to clothing, the only clothing that is truly holy is the robe of righteousness Christ has given us. He has the right to bless us in this way because he was clothed in our flesh. Our being clothed with his goodness is a clothing of the heart in humility and love for our neighbor. It is not about outward appearances that have absolutely no value against fleshly indulgences but rather stirs them up (Col. 2:20–23). If we are proud of the way we dress, whether fashionable or unfashionable, we're forgetting our true clothing. Modesty is primarily a matter of the heart and secondarily a matter of dress.

To protect our children's childlikeness is to protect their hearts and minds. They need to be reminded that love has been given to them by their Savior, and that is where their worth lies. Looking at how we live our lives, how we raise our children, and how we teach them to live gospel-centered lives through the lens of the One Good Story will take more thought and investment of time, conversations, and effort. A list is always so much easier, isn't it? But reciting the gospel, instilling its values in our children, and striving to live a life that reflects it will bear good, sweet fruit. It might be seen in our children's lives, in our lives, or beyond. It might become evident sooner or later. However the One Good Story is lived out, God is not done writing it. May that encourage us to guide our children with wisdom and offer grace as we all learn as we go.

Remembering God's Grace

Hopefully you feel empowered and have more confidence to guide your children as you see things through the lens of the One Good Story. Reflect and answer these questions, and ask the Holy Spirit to convict and teach you as you go.

1) What is the One Good Story? Recite it to yourself.

2) When making decisions about how to live out the gospel in our current culture in areas where Scripture offers no clear answers, in what areas do you most need help?

3) How does this chapter's take on media and modesty differ from what you were taught and what you've taught your children? How can the One Good Story change the way you teach your children to wisely engage in media and modesty?

PART 3

Grace for Today's Concerns

8

Grace When It Comes to Anxiety and Depression

For we do not have a high priest who is unable to empathize with our weaknesses, but we have one who has been tempted in every way, just as we are—yet he did not sin. Let us then approach God's throne of grace with confidence, so that we may receive mercy and find grace to help us in our time of need.

Hebrews 4:15–16

I (Jessica) admit that I am writing this chapter with much trepidation. While I have a child who suffers from mental illness and have been walking this road for many years, in some respects I feel less than qualified to write anything about mental illness. I personally have not struggled in this area, but I do see the effects of it. I have cried with my child countless times. I have watched them fight and triumph. Other times I have seen them too tired to fight and have marveled at their courage just to keep going. On my kiddo's eighteenth birthday, my child, a few trusted friends, and I went to a tattoo artist to get a semicolon tattoo together. Project Semicolon is a national mental health organization dedicated to raising awareness of and reducing the stigma of suicide and to providing resources for people with mental health experiences.[1]

The idea is that whenever you see that semicolon on your body (mine is on my right wrist), you remember that your story isn't over. It isn't the end. There is no period; instead, there is a semicolon. It is a sort of "I see you" to those who have experienced suicidal ideation and an "I am sorry" to those whose loved ones have succumbed to those dark thoughts. It is also a great reminder that our story keeps going, there is more to come, and hope is on the horizon. I can't tell you how many times I've looked down and seen my tattoo and known God was speaking to me through punctuation.

I recently saw a headline in an email from our local news station here in San Diego that stopped my scrolling and quite literally made me gasp. It said, "Rady Children's Hospital seeing 30% spike in children experiencing mental health crises. Doctors say some children as young as six have come to the emergency room with thoughts of suicide."[2] I had to read just that headline several times because I couldn't believe what I was seeing. Then, as I read the full article, I saw the news got much worse. While local physicians were seeing up to thirty children a day come in for mental health issues, this wasn't just something San Diego kids were experiencing. This 30 percent spike is happening across our nation. The CDC currently reports that 1 in 5 children have diagnosed mental health disorders and only about 20 percent of them are getting the treatment they need.[3] Our kids are in serious trouble and pain.

Mental health issues have been steadily increasing, according to the World Health Organization: "There has been a 13% rise in mental health conditions and substance use disorders in the last decade (to 2017)."[4] The questions parents, caregivers, and mental health workers everywhere are asking are, Where have all our happy children gone? Why are we seeing such dramatic increases in anxiety and depression? And, maybe most importantly, Have I done anything to contribute to this problem?

In 2019, I authored a book called *How to Help Your Anxious Teen: Discovering the Surprising Sources of Their Worries and Fears.* In it I looked at what I believed were reasons our kids were experiencing more anxiety and depression than in years past. I obviously had no idea the pandemic was about to start and would only exacerbate this already burgeoning problem. In that book, I propose that many factors have contributed to this rise in mental health issues, and here we will take a brief look at three of these—society, the church, and parents—and hopefully come up with a new way forward.

A Word of Caution

Before we start looking for answers, I want to caution parents not to try to solve your or your child's mental health issues alone. This chapter may bring some insights, but it would benefit you and your child to do more research and/or seek medical help. You may be hesitant to receive outside help, and I understand that hesitation. We never know what someone will say to our children, and it is our job to protect them. But we must acknowledge that there are some areas we are not equipped for, and we need those who have been trained to help us with our children. Don't wait to get the help you need.

Occasionally, we all feel anxious or depressed, and that may cause us to diminish what our children are feeling because we think we understand. But if your child is having trouble performing basic tasks, like getting out of bed for school, brushing their teeth, eating, or socializing with the family, it is imperative to get them help. If your child asks to see someone outside the family or even outside the church for their depression and anxiety, please listen to them. And if your child is talking to you about how they are struggling, consider yourself lucky. Lots of children won't share or will feel like they can't talk to their parents about what they are going through. If your child hasn't mentioned feeling anxious or depressed but you have suspicions they are feeling that way, why not just ask?

If your child does suffer from anxiety or depression, it has probably affected your life in one way or another. There are times we just want a quick fix or for our children to "get better." I know how hard it is and how your heart breaks for your child. But we must remember that we don't just need a fix for their issues; we need to learn to love them and sit with them in their pain. As we look at the way God loves us, we can learn to love our children in grace-filled, hope-filled ways.

He promises to be with you every step of the way. He promises to uphold you. He promises not to sleep on the job. You can trust him.

1. Society

Social Media

As we consider this rise in rates of anxiety and depression over the last fifteen years, we must ask ourselves what has changed. I am sure for most of us the first thing that comes to mind is the internet and the rise of social media use. Now, let me be clear: social media use does not make our kids anxious or depressed, but we can be certain it does contribute to depression and anxiety.[5] The comparison that happens on social media will work one of two ways in your kids' hearts—and, if we are honest, in our hearts as well. It will either create pride—"I am easily as cute as they are"—or anxiety or depression—"Why didn't I get invited to that party?" "I will never look that good." While social media may have been created with the intention of connecting people, it often has the opposite effect. The feeling of isolation follows prolonged periods of time spent there.

Social media has led to the disdain of the mundane and ordinary. When we scroll on our phones, we see all the exciting things our friends or family are taking part in while we sit at home wondering why our lives are so boring. We also see all the accomplishments of others and think that maybe we won't ever live up to our full potential—or, even worse, maybe we *are* living up to our full potential, and this is it.

Academics

Social media isn't the only thing contributing to this hatred for the ordinary. Our kids are encouraged as early as third grade to be thinking about what college they want to attend. There are grade schools that make children take tests and be interviewed before they are admitted. The college admission process is quite honestly out of control. Kids can have incredible GPAs, varsity sports stats to boast about, club leadership, and community service hours galore, and they still aren't getting into their preferred schools. In *Where You Go Is Not Who You'll Be*, author Frank Bruni says this:

> Somewhere along the way, a school's selectiveness—measured in large part by its acceptance rate—became synonymous with its worth. Acceptance rates are prominently featured in the profiles of schools that appear in various reference books and surveys, including the raptly monitored one by *U.S. News & World Report*, whose annual ranking of American colleges factor in those rates slightly. Colleges know that many prospective applicants equate a lower acceptance rate with a more coveted, special and brag-worthy experience, and these colleges endeavor to bring their rates down by ratcheting up the number of young people who apply. They bang the drums like never before. From the organization that administers the SAT, they buy the names of students who have scored above a certain mark and are at least remotely plausible, persuadable applicants, then they send those students pamphlets and literature that grow glossier and more alluring—that leafy quadrangle! those gleaming microscopes!—by the year. The college admissions

office is no longer a screening committee. It's a ruthlessly efficient purveyor of Ivory Tower porn.[6]

Society emphasizes the need to go to a school with a great reputation in order to get a great job, have lots of money, and live a great life. But there are many people who don't go to college at all and are very successful, many who go to trade schools and end up doing what they love for the rest of lives, and many who live modest lives but are happy, which should equal success. But in our society, we seem to think that *success* is defined by more time in college, more academic accolades, and more awards. The pressure to perform scholastically is taking a toll on our kids.

Sports

"Three out of four American families with school-aged children have at least one playing an organized sport—a total of about 45 million kids."[7] Perhaps this is true in your family too. Almost everyone is playing organized sports. I have nothing against kids playing sports, and I think it is beneficial on a lot of different levels. It can aid character building and be physically advantageous. But our national obsession with our kids playing sports is out of hand. Actually, let me rephrase that—our national obsession with kids *excelling* at sports is out of hand. If you have recently been to any youth sports games, you've probably heard other parents talking about their children with such a reverence you would think they were talking about professional athletes!

In every high school, a few kids stand out because they are great athletes. Kids wear their all-star gear everywhere they go. One of the first questions kids get asked is, "Do you play sports? Which ones?" The assumption is that most kids play several sports, and the older they get, the more they are inclined to put all their effort into excelling at just one. Is it because we are becoming a nation obsessed with getting our kids into good colleges? Is it because the fame and fortune of being a professional athlete are so alluring?

Or is it just because the magnetism of being better at something than others is all we can think about?

I know of several different high schools that bend the rules for their athletes. They don't abide by state regulations meant to ensure student athletes are getting the grades they should. These coaches think winning is more important than kids passing their English class. Perhaps they do not flat-out break the rules but "strongly encourage" other students on the team to "help" their teammate with their homework. Though the coach may not explicitly state it, the message is loud and clear: the star athlete must not be sidelined due to grades. There is even a trend to lower the 2.0 grade point average requirement so more kids can play.

The constant praise of athletic accomplishments communicates to our kids that their worth is tied up in how they perform on the field. The cultural worship of professional athletes communicates that fame and fortune are the pinnacles of human success. Of course, this creates anxiety. When a child fails—strikes out, fumbles the ball, misses the putt, or whatever—they feel the disappointment of everyone around them. Conversely, when they succeed, they have an inflated sense of accomplishment. Neither of these is a good thing. Part of the benefit of sports is to learn to be a team player and keep an even temperament whether you win or lose. This is a good life skill. But too much emphasis on performance will end in too much stress or anxiety for a kid.

Social Activism

Another prominent factor contributing to teen anxiety is the societal call to be involved in a greater cause. Again, this isn't necessarily a bad thing, but kids are being asked to fill their free time (as if they had a ton of free time, considering their sports and academic obligations) with volunteering.

Time magazine puts out a list every year of the thirty most influential teens. When I read through the past few lists, I felt incredibly inadequate. All my accomplishments in my forty-plus years of life seemed like nothing compared to some of these kids, who have multimillion-dollar companies or have raised awareness for noble causes.

The bigger the platform, the bigger the influence, the better off you are—that is the message from society. You need a message, and you need to shout it from the mountaintops (or your TikTok account). It's not just about making money; it's about being passionate about something that needs fixing. It's about the rise of social activism. Although the money received for views doesn't hurt at all.

The kids in Parkland, Florida, who survived the horrific Marjory Stoneman Douglas High School shooting of 2018 have used social media to organize gun control rallies. Several have tens of thousands of followers on X (formerly known as Twitter) alone. These are just a few of the teens who have used the tragedy to advance the fight for gun control. Imagine the pressure they must feel to stay relevant and make a difference.

This is not a commentary on their views or my own. Instead, I'm fascinated by the way social media has changed our culture and the pressure it can put on kids. The students affected by the Columbine school shooting in 1999 didn't have the platform to immediately express their concerns to the world. For Parkland kids, silence online was hardly an option. Please don't get me wrong. Speaking out against social injustices *is* a good thing, but the pressure to do it, to keep it up, to stay relevant, and to have a take on everything is contributing to anxiety.

Are We Safe?

When Elyse and I first wrote this book, gun violence was already an issue kids were having to process as they went to school. School shootings have only increased over the last decade, and it doesn't seem like there is any solution in sight. Now children are also having to think about being shot in movie theaters, big-box stores, churches, community parades, and on and on the list goes.

COVID-19 and the resulting shutdown of life as we knew it has also played a significant role in the rise of anxiety and depression in our children. In 2022, a study was released that showed, "In the first year of the COVID-19 pandemic, global prevalence of anxiety and depression increased by a massive 25%, according to a scientific brief released by the World Health Organization."[8] As adults we understand this, because we too were faced with a complete disruption to our lives.

The ongoing threat to safety and health has hurt our children in ways we don't even understand. And we won't understand the full effects for decades.

2. The Church

It is easy to look "out there" and identify the ways society is contributing to the rise of mental illness, but we must also turn our gaze inward and see how the church has contributed. In a moment we'll get into the messages the church lays on the backs of our kids that hurt them, but first we need to acknowledge that many churches don't even address mental illness in a helpful way. Lifeway did a study on the church's attitude toward mental illness and reported these findings.

- Only a quarter of churches (27 percent) have a plan to assist families affected by mental illness according to pastors. And only 21 percent of family members are aware of a plan in their church.
- Few churches (14 percent) have a counselor on staff skilled in mental illness or train leaders how to recognize mental illness (13 percent), according to pastors.
- Two-thirds of pastors (68 percent) say their church maintains a list of local mental health resources for church members. But few families (28 percent) are aware those resources exist.

- Family members (65 percent) and those with mental illness (59 percent) want their church to talk openly about mental illness, so the topic will not be taboo. But 66 percent of pastors speak to their church once a year or less on the subject.[9]

As we can plainly see, the church is just at the beginning of its journey to understanding mental illness and to know how to help its congregants. Because of this disconnect, the church is many times not only ill-prepared to help those in its care but also intolerant of those who experience mental illness. Often, we try to fix people with a Band-Aid verse, and we end up doing more harm than good.

"Do Big Things for God"

I grew up in the church, and I can't number the times I heard the message that I needed to be ready to "do big things for God." From a very young age, we hear about the "heroes" in the Bible and are encouraged to "be a Daniel, Esther, Ruth, Moses," and so on. We are constantly shown the bright spots of our heroes in the Bible and told to emulate them. I can't tell you how surprised I was when I learned the full story of each of these people, especially King David. Imagine my shock when I found out this "hero" also had a résumé full of lies, rape, and murder.

The pressure to do big things, to make a difference, to be a change maker is prevalent. I do wonder how often our kids hear about the big thing God has done for them in Christ or how God shows our community love through little things we do every day, like going to school, being kind to our neighbors, and seeing those who are typically unseen.

"Be a Good Christian"

We have already talked about the expectations we place on our kids to be "good" throughout this book. When they go to Sunday school or youth group, they hear the same message. The place that is supposed to provide relief ends up just putting more burdens on our kids' backs. In Matthew 11 Jesus says this: "Come to me, all you who are weary and burdened, and I will give you rest. Take my yoke upon you and learn from me, for I am gentle and humble in heart, and you will find rest for your souls. For my yoke is easy and my burden is light" (vv. 28–30). Do our kids hear that Jesus gives them rest? Or do they think they need to be doing the absolute most to gain his love and approval? I am afraid we've turned the good news into a way to control our kids' behavior, and in the process we've made them anxious and depressed.

3. Our Contribution

As parents, we contribute to our children's anxiety and depression by using them to build our own identity instead of loving them as who God created them to be. We take their accomplishments on the field or in the classroom and use those things to make ourselves feel like we are good parents. We hide ourselves in the doings of our children instead of the finished work of Christ. When the way our children look or the accolades they receive make us feel like we have really done something right, we are using our kids.

When we feel like a failure when they don't perform on the court, when we become unreasonably angry at a missed shot, when we feel shame because they missed a note during a piano recital, this is proof we are using our children. When we place our identity in their hands, we end up crushing our kids. I know this is a hard word. I can't tell you the number of times I've felt myself doing this. It is so easy to wrap up our whole identity into being a "good mom" or "proud dad," but we are expecting our children to do what only God can do for us. He alone gives us a rooted and grounded identity as his beloved.

Or maybe you are tempted to try to control everything in their lives so they never feel any negative emotion. You talk to their coaches or teachers or employers when they correct your children because you think they aren't being fair. You keep your children's lives full of activities and always have something fun or educational to do so they don't feel bored. When we do this, we are malforming our children. We must let them go through hard emotions and feel boredom so they learn lifelong skills on how to deal with those things. When we fix everything for our kids right away, we are stealing valuable lessons from them. Please, don't get me wrong: I am not saying to just throw your kids to the wolves and let them figure out life for themselves. What I am saying is that it would be good to ask yourself if you need to be so involved in every area of your kids' lives. Are there times you should or can step back and let them figure things out for themselves? When we constantly intervene, we are setting them up for failure when they are older and we're not around to help with everything. This is another reason for the higher rates of anxiety and depression. Parents have been overly involved in making life easy while kids are at home, and when they get out of the house, they find that life is not easy, and they don't know how to cope.

A Kind Word

Reading all of this might make you feel hopeless, anxious, or depressed. I know it is hard, and it seems like there is so much going against our kids. But I want to offer you a word of hope you can pass on to your kids. Proverbs 12:25 says this: "Anxiety weighs down the heart, but a kind word cheers it up." You and your kids need a kind word to lighten your loaded hearts. That kind word is that you are absolutely loved beyond measure.

My prayer is that, as you have read this chapter, you have seen anxiety and depression as complex and not just a "fix it and forget it" sort of problem. It isn't something to hide from and just pray it resolves itself. Stephanie Phillips, coauthor of *Unmapped*, shares how important this is:

I had always thought of anxiety as a sin to counter or a weakness to be overcome, but now I was hearing it was a legitimate condition, and the exposure of this condition within myself was setting me free. *Un-Shaming me.* There was a name for all the difficulty I battled on a moment-by-moment basis, I was far from alone. The shame slowly ebbed.[10]

I hope I've equipped you to see some of the causes of anxiety and depression, but I also hope you can see that you can't simply solve it. Don't add shame to the anxiety or depression your child is feeling. Don't put unneeded pressure on them to change. Just share with them what you know will be helpful, provide resources, offer to take them to see a professional counselor, and leave the change to the Holy Spirit. He is much better at it than you are. I promise.

We truly can trust and lean in to our heavenly Father's care for us. However, I want to be very clear that even though this is true, we are not prohibited from using other means to overcome anxiety or depression. In his inexhaustible grace and mercy, God has given us scientists who have invented helpful medications. He has given us doctors who have a desire to understand and help people who suffer from mental illness. He has given us professional counselors who long to sit and listen to and advise those who feel anxious or depressed. He has given us pastors who have committed their lives to taking care of God's people. He has given us youth pastors who look for ways to encourage our teens. All these gifts are here for us and our kids to obtain the help that is needed.

God has also given us ordinary means to help us walk through this life of trouble, fear, and sadness. One often overlooked way is living a life that involves a rhythm of rest. The Sabbath, however we choose to take it, is a way for us and our children to stop producing and working. It is a time or a day when we remind ourselves that we are human and need rest. Working a time of rest into a family's week is incredibly difficult, especially if we are ruled by sports or academics or performances. The constant call to produce, to be busy, adds to the anxiety and depression our kids may be feeling. Give them time to rest. Make a space for them to rest. I know of some families that have a special "rest" chair. Just a space in daily life where someone can go if they need a little time. Get creative with this! I also know some kids just aren't built to rest, and it will be hard for them to sit for any amount of time. When I homeschooled my kids, I would often read to them. During this time, I wouldn't ask them to sit completely still. I would allow them to draw or play with LEGOs, as long as they were able to tell me what I had read to them. Again, this is just what I did with my family. Involve your children in looking for a way for them to "rest" that works for your family.

As you reflect on this chapter in the context of this book, I hope you will not think that, now that you have some knowledge, you can solve your child's mental illness. Humbly recognize your limits and look outside of yourself. Pray the Holy Spirit will grant you the strength to admit you can't fix every problem. Pray for wisdom as you seek out a psychologist, therapist, or counselor. Be up-front with your pastor or other leaders from your church about what your family is going through. There is no need to pretend mental illness doesn't exist; it is detrimental to ignore it and hope it goes away. Drag it into the light where you can get help.

And lastly, remember the gospel, the good news that Jesus understands what it is like to live here on earth, in our bodies, with our minds, hearts, and emotions. Remember he is near, and he hates the brokenness mental illness causes.

We and our children can have a right standing with God not because of anything we have done but because of what he has done. We can know we are completely forgiven and forever be assured of God's love for us. He is working for the restoration of all things. This means our minds too. Our final home is with him, in a place where every anxious or depressing thought will be a distant memory and where all we will know is joy and peace forever.

Remembering God's Grace

If your child is dealing with anxiety or depression, the weight of parenting can become heavier. You are seen, and you are not alone. Take a few seconds right now to breathe deeply and slowly, inviting the Spirit to strengthen you, sustain you, and give you wisdom. Then, take some time to reflect on the following questions.

1) In what ways do you see society contributing to a child's anxiety or depression?

2) In your experience, how has the church ignored mental health concerns?

3) What are some ways your parenting might need to change in light of this chapter?

9

Raising Girls and Boys in Grace

Male and female are biological categories. Masculine and feminine are cultural categories.

Dorothy L. Sayers[1]

As we've noticed, there are very few verses in the New Testament that tell parents how to raise their children aside from training them in the message of the gospel. However, there are a few verses in the Old Testament (some of which we've already looked at in Proverbs) that have been used frequently by people who seek to construct a "biblical" method of parenting. Woven into many of these teachings are inferences about the differences between sexes (which are biological) and how children should be socialized into roles according to gender. In this chapter, we'll indeed affirm that there are two distinct biological sexes, male and female, and that, except in very rare intersex cases, children are assigned a male or female sex at birth. In addition, certain segments of Christianity also propose that children should be taught specific gender role expectations that conform to masculine and feminine stereotypes.[2] It's our goal in this chapter to clear up some of the confusion these stereotypes have caused.

Old Covenant Daughters and Sons

Under the old covenant, the law declared a differentiation between the ways boys and girls were thought of, treated, and raised. From the eighth day of life, boys were marked with circumcision, a sign "in the flesh" (Gen. 17:14) that declared they were part of the covenant community. Girls, on the other hand, could only be assured of their membership in that community by their relationship to a circumcised father, husband, or son. As those who received the covenant sign, sons alone were raised to lead the way in Israel's relationship with the Lord. They were taught that the obligation, responsibility, and privilege of national representation belonged to them and not to their sisters. They alone bore the mark of their faith in their flesh. They alone were trained to lead. Upon them alone was the burden to be Yahweh's representatives in the earth.

This is demonstrated throughout the Old Testament, as only sons are taught the obligations that came with their gender (see the book of Proverbs particularly). Of course, there are times of instruction (though comparatively few) that speak of "children" rather than "sons," but the preponderance is focused on male children. They were to be groomed to be the leaders, they alone could be priests, and they were God's representatives in the earth (see Gen. 12:1–3).

The life of a little girl under the old covenant was different. Although she was unlike girls in the Greco-Roman world, who were frequently abandoned to die at birth, and was welcomed into the household and faith, her value was always diminished. She didn't bear the sign. She could only be assured of her acceptance and inclusion in the covenant community by her relationship with a male who did. While she was young, she was taught her brothers had privileges not available to her. Every time a boy viewed his circumcised genitalia, he knew: *I belong to God.* A little girl could know nothing like that. Even as she matured and embraced the religion of her family, her identity would still be tied to her male relations, and then hopefully, if she was blessed, one day to sons of her own. Because of this, she needed to be taught from a young age how to care for a home because the home was where those males with the sign would reside and be raised.

As her father taught the family the Torah, she would learn that there were other differences between her and her brothers. When her mother birthed her, her mother would have been unclean for fourteen days. After her brothers were born, her mother was unclean for only seven days. Once a female began menstruating (a sign that she might be privileged to birth a son), she would be unclean for fourteen days (see Lev. 12). On the other hand, if males had a nocturnal emission, they would be unclean only until evening (Deut. 23:10).

Practically from day one of her life, she was taught to accept there was something different about her. She only had value in a secondary way. Aside from the exception brought about by the petition of Zelophehad's daughters (see Num. 27:1–9), she would not inherit anything of her father's. She was completely dependent on her male relatives for life and especially for her identity as a godly woman. She could be given in marriage to anyone her father chose. Her attractiveness, homemaking skills, femininity, and piety (demonstrated primarily by her virginity and ultimately by her fertility) were all she had to rely on to attract a prospective husband and live a life of respectability, free from destitution and shame. She could not initiate a divorce. Her entire value was tied to her reproductive system. She was even barred from the inner recesses of the synagogue in her village and the temple in Jerusalem. She was second class, and she knew it.

Because her brothers had different obligations and responsibilities, they needed to be trained in what passed for masculinity
at that time. They would be called to mediate as priests in their
homes. They might be called to go to war to protect their families,
so they needed to be trained in battle tactics. They were God's
representatives to their families and to the watching world. Sons
needed to be taught they were leaders. Daughters needed to be
taught they were followers.

Sons *and* Daughters Are Welcome Here

But all of this—and we mean *all* of it—changed when the covenant
sign of circumcision was replaced by the covenant sign of baptism.
Whether you hold to paedo or credo baptism is immaterial for
this discussion.[3] What matters is that daughters are welcomed
and treated with the same value and dignity as sons. The door
has been thrown open. When the curtain in the temple was torn
at Christ's death, it was torn for both boys *and* girls. The "Keep
out!" sign was demolished, and "All are welcome!" replaced it.

Girls could now bear the sign of inclusion in the new covenant
family, the church. They could be baptized. Like their brothers,
girls were now accorded the full rights of adoption, inheritance,
instruction, and citizenship (see Rom. 8:29; Gal. 4:28; 1 Thess.
1:4; 4:1; 5:27). Girls could approach the throne room of God in
prayer (2 Thess. 3:1; Heb. 10:19) because they bore the mark of
entrance into the community of believers: baptism. They would
also be filled with the Spirit, enabled and commissioned to speak
truth about the kingdom of God (Acts 2:17). The Old Testament's exclusively male priesthood was ended and superseded
by the priesthood of all believers (1 Pet. 2:9). Of course, females
still needed a relationship with a circumcised, baptized male, and
they had it: they were sisters of their elder brother, Jesus Christ
(Heb. 2:17). Along with their brothers, they were equally part of
his bride.

Sons and daughters of God would equally be called to faith and to follow Jesus into the water (Matt. 3:14). And when girls and boys would wonder, from time to time, whether they were really his, they could remember their baptism. They had been indelibly marked as his. Their gender would no longer exclude them nor give them special privilege.

Way too much of what is commonly taught as "Christian" methods of parenting for daughters and sons completely misses the realities these changes established with the inclusion of girls in the new covenant sign of baptism, the infilling by the Spirit of both boys and girls, and the priesthood of all believers. Once we grapple with these momentous changes in status from the old to the new covenant, we'll begin to rightly question whether gender teachings that rely so heavily on Old Testament narratives and stereotypes are Christian at all.

There simply are *no* commands in the new covenant about what to teach daughters that differ in any way from what is required for sons. Daughters are to be taught to love and care for their families. So are sons. Daughters are to be taught to be pure and modest. So are sons. Daughters are to be taught to be devout. So are sons. Daughters are to be taught to use their gifts for the community of the faith. So are sons. Way too much is drawn from the old covenant about what it means to raise masculine sons and feminine daughters. Far too many girls have been made to feel that their only option and entire worth as human beings is tied to finding a husband and giving birth. Far too many boys have been pushed into "manly" activities (whether they liked them or not). This really must stop.

Of course, again, one reason so much teaching in parenting is drawn from the Old Testament is because the New Testament is nearly silent on specific methods for child training. What we do find in the New Testament are records of many women who had callings and ministries to the entire family of God. Jesus welcomed and partnered with them. Paul honored and employed them.

Churches were founded in their homes. They had ministries of great importance to the church. An unmarried European woman, Lydia, led the way for all her sisters and brothers into the kingdom of God. Marriage, though good if that is one's inclination and God's design, is just one option for believing women.

Gospel-Loving Daughters and Sons

What does it look like to raise children who are trained in the gospel? In a nutshell, it looks like teaching them the many truths we've talked about in this book. There isn't a particular teaching for boys and a different one for girls. There's no place where parents are told to make sure their daughters know how to wash windows and their sons know how to load a rifle. Sons and daughters are equally in need of hearing the good news. The Word only says "do not exasperate your children; instead, bring them up in the training and instruction of the Lord" (Eph. 6:4).

We must wonder whether at least part of the pushback to modern American evangelicalism we're hearing from exvangelicals[4] is the outworking of the exasperation (Col. 3:21) and stirring up of the anger (Eph. 6:4) Paul warned about. If all these people heard as children about Christianity had to do with being nice, being polite, voting a certain way, and following certain midcentury gender stereotypes, then we understand their angst. Way too many girls are reacting against stereotypical straitjacketing that plans out their whole lives without reference to their inclinations, giftings, weaknesses, strengths, or even God's design. Far too many boys are reacting against a toxic masculinity that demeans them if they're not "manly" enough (What even is that?) and are tired of striving to live up to expectations that deny their emotional development and appreciation of beauty.

The deadly dysfunction in Isaac's family is a perfect picture of two types of masculinity and what happens when parents favor one over the other.

> When the boys grew up, Esau became an expert hunter, an out-
> doorsman, but Jacob was a quiet man who stayed at home. Isaac
> loved Esau because he had a taste for wild game, but Rebekah loved
> Jacob. (Gen. 25:27–28 CSB)

You likely know the end of the story: the parents' favoritism even-
tuated in conflict and the rupturing of the family.

The gospel teaches us that each of our children have been created in the image of God and are being re-created in the image of
the Son as unique individuals with unique gifts and inclinations.
Perhaps one child's predisposition will align more closely with
your own. Perhaps not. Let's just be careful not to assume that the
propensity that appeals to us means they're godlier. As much as
they could take after us, they're unique to themselves, and that's
a wonderful thing.

We're not saying that one way of expressing gender is better
than another. We're not saying that staying home reading books
is better than being outdoorsy. Nor are we saying that a woman
who chooses an academic career is better than one who stays home
to raise children. What we are saying is that any stereotypical
straitjacketing of gender *in any way* is harmful, exasperating, dis-
heartening, and completely unbiblical. Our children don't need
to be taught how to be masculine or feminine. This isn't Sparta
or Athens. This is the New Jerusalem, and our children need to
be taught the life-giving, soul-nourishing freedom of justification
through faith in Christ alone.

Hearts Shaped by the Gospel

Our children must be taught the truth that their siblings and
friends, whether male or female, have value because they are
made in God's image. What that means is that boys should be
taught they aren't better, godlier, or of greater value than girls. Of
course, the opposite is true too. Girls need to be taught that their

brothers and male friends are God's precious creation and not to be denigrated simply because they're male. There is no place for misogynistic teachings about all girls needing to submit to all boys or girls only having value if boys like them. There is also no place for misandrist teachings that disrespect God's image in boys or assume that they're all selfish bullies or uncaring brutes.

Girls and boys need to be taught to welcome and love one another, not simply because they may be members of the same biological family but because they are members of an eternal and more glorious one: the family of God. Sometimes that means girls will welcome their little brothers into their play, and vice versa, with never even a whisper of "No boys/girls allowed." Of course, sometimes children of the same gender love to play together, and we don't want to say that should never happen. It's just that no child should be taught they're automatically excluded from "all the fun stuff" simply because of their gender.

Like their parents, children do need to be taught how to defer to one another in humility. Ephesians 5:21 says, "Submit to one another out of reverence for Christ." Of all the things parents need to both teach and learn ourselves, this may be the most difficult. No one likes to relinquish control. We certainly don't like to think others are more important than ourselves (Phil. 2:3). The only way to be free from our innate desire to be the boss or make sure everything goes the way we want is by soaking our souls in the humility and condescension of our elder brother, Jesus. He's the only one who can assure us we'll be okay even if others are guiding the conversation, direction, or activity. After all, "He who did not spare his own Son, but gave him up for us all—how will he not also, along with him, graciously give us all things?" (Rom. 8:32). And because he promised that he "richly provides us with everything for our enjoyment" (1 Tim. 6:17), we can learn to release control and, as the kids might say, "Just chill."

Neither boys nor girls should be taught they should always be in charge simply because of their gender. Boys should never be taught their sisters should acquiesce to their demands and serve them just because of their gender. Girls should never be taught they have to do what boys tell them to—or to always try to be in charge because they are girls. Nor should they be taught they are responsible for the sins of the boys around them. We all have enough of a burden to recognize and repent of our own sins; girls don't need to take on the responsibility of the sins their brothers struggle with. Both brothers *and* sisters need to learn to "clothe [themselves] with the Lord Jesus Christ" and not "think about how to gratify the desires of the flesh" (Rom. 13:14). Humility of heart is not something any of us learns easily or by nature. It is a function of continuous pursuit of faith in Christlikeness.

Thinking too highly of ourselves is endemic (12:3). Although it is good to teach our children to value themselves as made in God's image, they should also be taught the dangers of thinking they are better than others. The result of this kind of Christless thinking results in conflict with others—the fight for preeminence, the fight to be boss, the fight to prove that one is in the right. As Paul writes, "Everyone should look not to his own interests, but rather to the interests of others" (Phil. 2:4 CSB). If all our children care about are their own interests, there will never be unity in the family or healthy relationships in community with others. James asks,

> What is the source of wars and fights among you? Don't they come from your passions that wage war within you? You desire and do not have. You murder and covet and cannot obtain. You fight and wage war. (James 4:1–2 CSB)

The Greek word translated "passions" in this passage means "a state or condition of experiencing pleasure for any reason, pleasure, delight, enjoyment, pleasantness."[5] The New Living

Translation of verse 1 reads, "What is causing the quarrels and fights among you? Don't they come from the evil desires at war within you?" The reason children squabble and fight is that they have selfish desires. They want to be boss. Brothers and sisters both want to enjoy the pleasure of controlling what others do. This desire, as James says, is anything but godly.

Sadly, some boys are taught that it is their place, just by virtue of their gender, to be in authority. Since there is no passage in Scripture that teaches that all males at all times are to be in charge, and since the very desire to want things our own way is evil, this teaching creates only conflict. Again, perhaps this is what we're seeing with exvangelicals. Of course, it is also destructive to teach girls to fight for preeminence—though we don't see much of that in typical Christian fare. There's a place in God's kingdom for Deborahs and for Abigails, for Esthers, for Hannahs, and for Marys (all of them).

God will call some of our children into positions of leadership, and that is good. It's good to train them to accept responsibility with humility and diligence. And it's especially good to teach them that leadership isn't based on gender.

If we're to be gospel-centered moms and dads who train gospel-centered girls and boys, we'll want them to learn what it means to be devoted to the building up and encouragement of others. We want them to experience the joy of watching others flourish. We might ask our sons, "What could you do today to encourage your sister to remember she is loved by God?" We might ask our daughters, "How could you show your brother how important he is to the Lord today?" We might say to all of our children, "You know there is real power in the words you say. You could help your siblings believe they can follow the Lord. What do you see in them that shows you they have gifts God could use?" That might take a little convincing and probably more than a little training, but think how worthwhile it would be for them to hear words of encouragement from one another.

Gospel-Centered Daughters

Gracious parenting looks like training girls to love and appreciate their bodies; that outward beauty, strength, and gifting are not the measure of their worth; and that though the Lord may indeed gift them with a husband and children, that's not their highest calling. Their highest calling is to love the Lord. They are free from any stereotype they may have heard about what Christian girls are supposed to be like.

In the paragraphs to follow, we'll be discussing some responses to cultural stereotypes that may or may not resonate with you and your family. Since God has gendered your daughters as female, they can ask the Lord to help them learn to love their bodies. Rather than feeling jealous of boys and their strengths, they can ask for wisdom to see the goodness of being female. As they mature and begin to change, they can see what is frequently a painful monthly difficulty as a way for the Lord to teach them what he knows about suffering and about how giving life to others always comes at a cost.

We understand how hard this might be for some. It appears that boys get to go through life more easily. They get to go out without their shirts on when it's hot. They don't have to wear bras or be expected to dress modestly all the time. They don't have to worry as much about being attacked when walking alone. They don't have to carry feminine products with them or try to figure out how to get to a toilet in time. They don't have to stay out of the pool or worry about an accident because they're menstruating. In addition, boys don't feel the same pressure to appear a certain way by worrying about how their hair looks or wearing makeup. And they seem to excel more easily at games or sports and are more frequently chosen to lead, whether they deserve it or not. Accepting their own worth while fighting envy and bitterness toward what seems to be an easier life is part of the struggle of being a woman in this world. Yes, in some ways, being a woman is a more difficult road. But knowing that the Lord is loving and good and has only good plans for his daughters can help. As you read through the Gospels, take time to notice how Jesus interacted with women. For instance, Luke 8 tells us that there were women who regularly traveled with Jesus and the disciples. In John 4, we learn of his love for a Samaritan woman to whom he reveals himself as the Messiah.[6]

Because God values all our bodies and sees them as beautiful for his purposes, our daughters can learn to live that way. They can live with self-respect. Our daughters need to understand this: contrary to much teaching in what's known as "purity culture," virginity is not the most important thing about them.[7] Not by a long shot. The most important thing is believing that they belong to our loving Savior and walking with him in faith and humility through all pain, sins, follies, and missteps. And when they question whether their faith is sufficient, they can remember they bear the sign of the new covenant on their bodies.

Where Does a Girl's Value Come From?

It's very difficult for girls to believe they have value if they don't fit a certain mold. For instance, a daughter might struggle if she's not very pretty (by worldly standards) or if she's clumsy, uncoordinated, or "throws like a girl." Maybe she's happiest when she's got her nose stuck in a book or when she doesn't have to think about how she looks. Other girls really love working out or getting their makeup done and shopping for a new outfit. Whatever your daughters' giftings or inclinations, the way in which they dress or engage their interests does not make them valuable or feminine. They are valuable because God created them as female. They are feminine for the same reason. You can let them find their own way as girls, giving them gentle guidance when they might be tempted to obsess over their beauty or size. You can gently remind them that true beauty doesn't consist of outward things like elaborate hairstyles or wearing gold jewelry or fine clothes, but rather what is inside the heart—the imperishable quality of a gentle and quiet spirit, which is of great worth in God's sight. (1 Pet. 3:3–4 CSB)

By the way, having a "gentle and quiet spirit" is not the same thing as what is usually called femininity. It doesn't mean to never call out wrong nor speak above a whisper. Nor does it mean to be weak. What it does mean is that we don't try to wrest control for situations or demand our own way. Rather, we trust in the Lord's goodness in all things.

Relationships with Boys Don't Bestow Worth

Too many girls are taught, either in their home, church, or culture, that their worth is bestowed by the opinion of males. They're taught that they don't have value unless they're in a relationship, and this only gets worse as they get older. Rather than teaching our daughters that their worth comes from pleasing their fathers (as is found in some patriarchal homes)[8] or from their boyfriends (as is found in the culture), we can assure them they have value simply because they have been created in the image of God and are members of the household of faith. Jesus gives them value because he loves them.

Giving Birth Doesn't Bestow Value

It may or may not be God's plan for your daughter to produce children. If it is, that's good. If it isn't, that's also good. What is important is that she seeks to fulfill the Great Commission—making disciples and teaching them the gospel. Perhaps your daughter will want to play with baby dolls and loves holding little children. Perhaps not. Her pathway is her pathway, not yours, to fashion. There are women who by inclination simply don't want to have children. There are others who want nothing more. Either or anything in between is perfectly acceptable.

The kingdom of God is open before believing daughters. None of the passages concerning spiritual gifts from Romans or 1 Corinthians are gendered. None of the passages about virtue are gendered. A woman might pursue a doctorate degree in English literature, or she might spend her mornings reading *The Jesus Storybook Bible* to her babies. She might get up early to train with the men in her unit, or she might teach in a preschool. God's kingdom and his gifts, callings, and welcome are open to her now, and she is to spend her days seeking to fulfill the Great Commission by loving her neighbors. Insisting that our daughters fulfill stereotypical gender roles from the 1950s or from Victorian England is unkind and may work at cross-purposes to God's call on their lives. Guide your daughter to love Jesus and his kingdom and seek to fulfill his plan for her, whatever that may be.

Gospel-Centered Sons

What does it look like to train our sons to be like Christ? First, it means that we teach them to love and appreciate their bodies. They have been made male, and maleness is good.

As boys mature, their bodies have male hormones that incline them to grow and act in certain ways. Boys must be taught to use their strength for the upbuilding of God's kingdom and for the good of those who do not have the strength they do. As they struggle with sexual desires, they must learn to keep this in proper perspective, remembering that sex is designed by God to serve the other (and not to please themselves alone).

Neither strength nor good looks are the measure of any boy's worth. Since the Bible commands us to care for our bodies, we should all strive to find an exercise that fits our needs, as we have the time or the inclination.[9] Being buff or being flabby are simply not the measure of a man's worth or masculinity. Health is important, but as Paul says, it's of "little value" in comparison to godly character (1 Tim. 4:8).

In the same way that their sisters are not to be defined by relationships with males, they are not defined by their relationships with females. Men can and should value women (no matter how they look outwardly) for their relationship with the Lord and their godly character. Contrary to toxic popular teaching, men can appreciate true beauty and turn from competition. Relationships with females are not the measure of their worth. Boys have value simply because they have been created in the image of God and are members of the household of faith, just like girls.

Having a family or career doesn't give them value. Some boys will love color and fabric and want to be interior designers. Other boys won't notice if they're wearing two different socks when they roll out of bed and pick up their surveying tools. Some men love to work outside, landscaping, while others delight in working in a classroom with children. Others love to ride waves or horses or drive Formula One cars. It's all good.

Boys are free to follow their gifts and inclinations in pursuit of the kingdom of God and its goal of discipleship among the nations. Some will love to lead. Many will not. Boys don't have to lead according to traditional expectations. They can be an example of what it means to follow Jesus in humility and lead by pursuing unity with those around them. They can grow in masculinity by adopting an attitude of curiosity and learning and not assuming they always have to have all the right answers. They can learn to embrace humility and the ability to say they are wrong. Whether they have been gifted with a brain that loves math or a brain that loves beauty, a heart that delights in trains or a heart that is moved by music, they must be taught and encouraged that they are uniquely crafted and can use their entire minds, bodies, and souls to love their God. The goal is never to seek to be culturally "manly" but rather to be like Christ, who is strong in the face of evil and yet welcomes children onto his lap and values relationships with the broken and powerless. Jesus is never concerned about what others think but walks courageously into all his Father's will.

As we close this chapter on raising gospel-loving boys and girls, here's our bottom line: aside from very specific instructions about biological functions, both genders are equally welcomed into God's family and are to be welcomed by one another without prejudice. There is no place in Christ's kingdom for either misogyny or misandry. We are to love our differently gendered neighbors as ourselves, all for the glory of the Son who was made "fully human in every way" (Heb. 2:17), just like his brothers and sisters.

What about Trans Kids?

Since a number of good books have already been written to help us understand and aid kids who struggle with gender dysphoria, I won't try to say everything that might and should be said here.[10]

I am aware this topic is a hot-button issue for many parents. I know that many parents view transitioning as the most terrifying danger they and their children might face. I also know many parents are walking through the confusion and heartbreak that go along with children who are struggling with gender or who have chosen to transition.

Since at this point it is impossible to know with complete certainty why some children struggle with gender and whether gender dysphoria has any sort of biological cause or is solely a result of societal pressure (or something in between), we should approach every interaction with humility and grace.[11]

When we talk about this issue, it's imperative to remember that gender dysphoria is not just an "issue." It involves *people*. It involves parents who have wept for their children and children who feel as though they are drowning in confusion and shame. We must remember that these parents and their children are people who have been created by God and are, like us all, filled with the desire to love and to live in the light of who they believe they are. These kids are, above all, children we need to love and seek to help. And many of them are already dealing with mental health issues, which makes this struggle even more painful.[12] As Preston Sprinkle writes,

> Correct science and correct theology are pointless if we're not willing to love and honor, listen to, and learn from, care for and be cared for by the trans people God has gifted us with.[13]

The "Law" of Gender Roles

One final word: as we have been saying throughout this book, the way the human heart naturally responds to the imposition of rules or law is to refuse to obey, to go the other way (see Rom. 7). If a child is continually taught they need to be masculine or feminine as defined by stereotypical Victorian gender expectations, we shouldn't be surprised if they resist and run in the other direction. We must avoid straitjacketing our daughters and sons with certain gender roles that fit into our social structures but may not fit their personality, gifting, temperament, and calling. In fact, the more we push against young peoples' desire to express themselves in atypical ways, the more they will run toward those ways.

Don't misunderstand. I'm not saying that *all* young people who struggle with gender dysphoria do so because they're responding to stringent teaching on gender roles. However, there is a possibility that some, especially those who struggle with rapid-onset gender dysphoria, may be.

I will also say that those who are predisposed to atypical modes of thinking and acting from a very early age should be encouraged that this doesn't mean they are wrongly sexed but rather are uniquely gifted and may be called by God to a vocation that needs a different sort of person to accomplish it. The prophetess and judge Deborah probably didn't fit in with many other women in her town. And when David was spending time writing songs, his brothers might have thought he was too feminine—until he killed Goliath, that is.

If one of your children seems to be struggling with any sort of gender dysphoria, let me encourage you to start praying and reading but also, above all, to keep listening and loving. Seek to understand what they might be facing and don't just respond with demands for change. Seek to love them and remind them of the good news: they are beloved and welcomed. And the Lord will walk with them throughout their difficult journey. And he will walk with you.

We're living in a time of great confusion and fear, especially about gender. The good news is that this time is not so different from every other time, although perhaps people are more vocal about this issue now. In any case, the Lord is powerful enough and wise enough to help you with all the questions and even the difficult times when it seems he's absent.

Remembering God's Grace

There's so much to unpack from this chapter, and there may have been points at which you felt challenged or uncomfortable. One of the best things you can do is bring those things before the Lord in prayer. Asking the Holy Spirit to guide you, answer these questions to reflect on the chapter.

1) How has your understanding of gender roles been shaped by Old Testament narratives that fail to recognize the changes in the new covenant?

2) Do you have any children who don't seem to fit into typical conservative Christian gender roles? How have you sought to love and encourage them? How can you encourage them to fulfill the unique call God has on their lives?

_____

_____

3) How has your understanding of the trans community been shaped by popular culture or by fear? How can you reframe your understanding to be shaped by love?

_____

_____

PART 4

Grace for Parents

10

Parenting through Prayer

The knowledge of God's Father-love is the first and simplest, but also the last and highest lesson in the school of prayer.

Andrew Murray[1]

Practically everyone has an "Aunt Biddy" sort of person in their lives. You know, she's the relative your parents had to tell you to be nice to. She's also the one who has the inheritance, so you know it's to your advantage to be nice and visit her . . . but it's just so hard. It's hard because you know that she doesn't really approve of you. She always sighs when you come in, and you know she'll tell your mother about all your miscues after you leave. And even though you know she has the resources to help you out when you get into a jam, you're loath to ask her because she'll sniff at you even more and make you grovel a little and explain why it is that you need her help . . . again.

On the other hand, when my grandkids come over on family night, they run into the house and hug me, and every one of them wants to talk to me at the same time. I (Elyse) used to have to shoo them out of the kitchen while I was making dinner because they wanted to watch and help and jabber. They each had a story to share, and frequently I had to listen to two or three of them at once. I'm Mimi, not Aunt Biddy!

The difference between the relationships we each have with our own personal "Aunt Biddy" and the relationship my grandchildren have with their Mimi can be summed up in one word: *love*. These little darlings know I love them and am delighted when they walk through the door. Love makes all the difference in their comfort level with me. I don't sniff at them; I draw them close and snuggle them. They are assured of my love, so they run toward me and jump on my lap and tell jokes and stories and ask for candy. They share their sorrows. They know I'll listen. They're comfortable with me and love me because they know that I love them.

Praying to Aunt Biddy

When it comes to prayer, most of us simply feel guilty. We know we should pray. We know we should present our requests to God. But for most of us (and for our kids), if we're honest, we'll admit that praying to God is a little like visiting with cranky old Aunt Biddy. Of course, theologically we know that's not the truth and that "God is love" (1 John 4:8), but at heart we're not really sure our prayers amount to anything more than lifeless protocol demanded by a disappointed father who sniffs at us, disapproves, and exacts some sort of obeisance before he opens up the bank vault to pinch out a little trinket from his treasures. Run into his presence? Raid the fridge? Ask to do our laundry? Ask for candy? With God? Hardly. How could we possibly think about him in that way? After all, he isn't our Mimi. He's the holy God, Lord of heaven and earth, who understands every thought and intention in our hearts. "Nothing in all creation is hidden from God's sight. Everything is uncovered and laid bare before the eyes of him to whom we must give account" (Heb. 4:13). Have an open and loving conversation with him? How?

In this chapter, Jessica and I are going to encourage you to take a look at the role of prayer in parenting.

Every Christian knows we have been commanded to pray, but our prayer life is frequently cold and lifeless. It tends to be just another chore on our daily checklist. Most of us don't have the same enthusiasm about it as we would have if we were going to visit a beloved friend whose generosity always amazes us. Our time in prayer is frequently more like a visit to Aunt Biddy. We tend to dread it or be lazy about it because we're not thrilled about spending time with God. And so, we often discover that our plan to pray—once we get the kids settled, once the morning routines are done, once the house is back to order—is thwarted yet again. Could it be that our aversion to prayer is caused by trying to motivate ourselves to pray through guilt? Guilt will never eventuate in sincere prayer. Guilt never motivates us to do anything wildly loving.

Praying to Your Loving Father

This is the one chief thought on which Jesus dwells; he would have us see that the secret of effectual prayer is *to have a heart filled with the Father-love of God*. It is not enough for us to know God is a Father: he would have us come under the full impression of what that name implies. We must take the best earthly father we know; we must think of the tenderness and love with which he regards the request of his child, the love and joy with which he grants every reasonable desire; we must then, as we think in adoring worship of the infinite love and fatherliness of God, consider how with much more tenderness and joy he sees us come to him, and gives us what we ask aright. And then, when we see how much this divine arithmetic is beyond our comprehension, and feel how impossible it is for us to apprehend God's readiness to hear us, then he would have us come and open our heart for the Holy Spirit to shed abroad God's father-love there.[2]

What praying parents need is a deep drink of the great love of God, our Father, not more commands to pray. You know you should pray about your parenting. Do you know how he loves you? Wrapping your head around his love for you will change your prayer time from visits with Aunt Biddy to family dinners with Mimi. The Lord isn't disappointed in you or in your parenting. He's not disappointed in your prayers. He doesn't get disappointed with his dear children. He doesn't want you to keep your distance, sitting in time-out until you learn your lessons. He invites you to come boldly in with joy and confidence. How are you, an imperfect parent and human, able to do that? Because the Son prays and intercedes for each of us! Because the Father loves us! Take a few moments to meditate on the verses below and ask the Spirit to give you faith to believe that Jesus's prayer and entreaty are powerful enough to change you and your children. Because of Jesus, your Father delights to hear the sound of your voice the same way I love to hear my grandchildren's voices—except exponentially more so.

> [Jesus] poured out his life unto death,
> and was numbered with the transgressors [that's us!].
> For he bore the sin of many,
> and made intercession for the transgressors. (Isa. 53:12)

Therefore he is able to save completely those who *come to God* through him, because he *always lives to intercede for them*. (Heb. 7:25)

For Christ did not enter a sanctuary made with human hands that was only a copy of the true one; he entered heaven itself, now to appear *for us* in God's presence. (9:24)

For there is one God and one mediator between God and mankind, *the man Christ Jesus, who gave himself as a ransom for all people.* (1 Tim. 2:5–6)

My dear children, I write this to you so that you will not sin. But if anybody does sin, *we have an advocate [intercessor] with the Father*—Jesus Christ, the Righteous One. (1 John 2:1)

Have you ever had the experience of gaining admittance into a private event because you were with someone who had an in? I have. It's nice to walk up to the stern guards at the door and say, "I'm with them," and then watch the guards' faces soften into welcome as they open the door wide. Here's the truth: when you walk into the throne room of the holy King of the universe, Jesus is standing by your side. You can simply say, "I'm with him," and all of heaven is at your disposal.

When we forget who we're with and who is interceding for us, we start to think we have to get our act together before God is interested in hearing from us. When that happens, we do all sorts of foolish things like boast about who is the greatest. Here's how Paul speaks peace to our hearts:

> So then, no more boasting about human leaders! *All things are yours*, whether Paul or Apollos or Cephas or the world or life or death or the present or the future—*all are yours, and you are of Christ, and Christ is of God*. (1 Cor. 3:21–23)

All things are ours! Every answer to prayer that we need is ours! When we soak our souls in the grace of the gospel, we'll find our desire to spend time with the Lord in prayer changing. We'll be more comfortable in our set times of prayer, and we'll also begin to carry on a nonstop conversation with him in our hearts because we know he loves to hear our voices. And then, when we're faced with a difficult decision or when the kids are fighting or need correction, we'll be comfortable running to him. *Lord, I know you're here. Help me see you. Give me grace*, will be our frequent heart's cry. Because the Holy Spirit *loves* to make Jesus grand in our eyes, he'll nurture, train, and remind us of his graciousness. And when we forget the gospel, he'll gently correct us and make Jesus appear grand to us again.

Are the kids making you a little crazy today? Remember you can pray, "I know you're with me, Lord, and you have given everything to me. Please help me see you now."

You can also have confidence when you pray because your heavenly Father loves you—yes, *you* personally. He loves you. Why? Because you're in the Son he loves, and because he has chosen to set his love upon you. Why? I don't know. When my grandchildren ask me why I love them, I don't get out my list of all the things they do that make them worthy of my love. I simply say, "Because you're *you*, and I love you." In a way, that's how it is with your heavenly Father, but he's been loving you since before there was a "you" to love. Ephesians 1:4 says, "He chose us in him before the creation of the world . . . in love." He was able to look down through all the corridors of time and see each of us and say, "I love him; I love her." Here's how the apostle John wrote about God's incomprehensible love for us:

> In that day you will ask in my name. I am not saying that I will ask the Father on your behalf. No, *the Father himself loves you* because you have loved me and have believed that I came from God. (John 16:26–27)

> My prayer is not for them alone. I pray also for those who will believe in me through their message . . . I in them and you in me— so that they may be brought to complete unity. Then the world will know that you sent me and have *loved them even as you have loved me.* (17:20, 23)

> See what great love the Father has lavished on us, that we should be called children of God! And that is what we are! (1 John 3:1)

No wonder Paul prayed that we might be given the ability to comprehend the incomprehensible: God's love for us in Christ. We'll never get to the end of this. We'll never plumb the depths of his love. Even in eternity we'll be surprised by grace every single day. Paul prayed that we "may have power, together with all the Lord's holy people, to grasp how wide and long and high and deep is the love of Christ, and to know this love that surpasses knowledge" (Eph. 3:18–19). In light of all our unbelief, it really does take the strength of God to believe God loves us. When we begin to grow in this confidence, a confidence that comes from grace, not our own works, we'll grow in our desire to pray too. He isn't Aunt Biddy. He's your loving Father. Here are precious words from Andrew Murray:

> In all the compassion with which a father listens to his weak or sickly child, in all the joy with which he hears his stammering child, in all the gentle patience with which he bears with a thoughtless child, we must, as in so many mirrors, *study the heart of our God's readiness to hear us*, then He would have us come and open our heart for the Holy Spirit to shed abroad God's Father-love there.[3]

Desperation Creates Praying Parents

Aside from questioning whether our Father really loves us and wants to hear our prayers, another reason we don't pray is because we're not really desperate. If we've been lulled into complacency and self-reliance because we have compliant children today, we probably won't feel much of a need to pray. As Paul Miller, author of *A Praying Life*, admits,

> It took me seventeen years to realize I couldn't parent on my own. It was not a great spiritual insight, just a realistic observation. If I didn't pray deliberately and reflectively for members of my family by name every morning, they'd kill each other. I was incapable of getting inside their hearts. I was desperate. But even more, I couldn't change my self-confident heart. . . . [I came to realize that] I did my best parenting by prayer. I began to speak less to the kids and more to God. It was actually quite relaxing.[4]

The Lord is kind to us in order to make us desperate for him. But frequently, when we feel desperate, we don't pray. We get out our books and try to figure out what we're doing wrong instead of falling on our knees and pleading with our Father. We double down on our efforts to get the kids to do our bidding, and we feel like we don't have time for prayer.

I know that being a busy parent can make anyone feel like they just don't have time to pray. *Pray? I can barely breathe!* Even if that's the case, if you ask for grace, the Lord will enable you to carry on a nonstop conversation with him in your heart all day long. *Lord, please grant us mercy now. Lord, I need your grace to respond to their bickering with gentleness now. Lord, please give me wisdom to see the cross in this.* These kinds of unspoken prayers will help you begin to rely more on him than on yourself.

Now, Pray Like Missionaries

The remembrance of Christ's intercession, our Father's love for us, and our desperation are the fuel we need to build the fire of fervent prayer in our hearts. Guilt won't do it. Laws about it will only crush us or make us self-righteous like the Pharisee in Luke 18. What we need is grace. We need grace to see God everywhere, to lavish grace on our children. So, as we talk now about how to pray for our parenting and how to pray for our children, remember, "we only maintain that our confidence cannot rest on anything else than the mercy of God alone."[5]

All Christian parents are missionaries. We are all on a mission from the Lord to announce the love of the Father to our children and to encourage them, as much as we can, to believe it. We're to tell them of the law so that they know they need rescue, and then we're to tell them of the Rescuer who has freed them from the law's curse. But this monumental task is utterly impossible for us to accomplish on our own. We, too, need both rescue and the Rescuer. And so we need to pray for help.

What follows are some examples of the prayers that another missionary, Paul, prayed. They will enlighten and direct our prayers away from the kinds of prayer that we're tempted as parents to pray—"Lord, just make them behave!"—to those that more clearly reflect our mission as Christ's representatives. Paul's prayers to the different churches have similar patterns. As we explore these patterns, we can learn how to pray for our personal mission field.

I (Jessica) have learned that the first section of Paul's prayers are always filled with thankfulness for the people to whom he is writing. He simply gushes with thanksgiving, speaking of his love for these people in astounding terms. Listen to the warm language he uses with his family in Philippi: "I yearn for you all with the affection of Christ Jesus" (Phil. 1:8 ESV). Paul longs to see the Thessalonians and wonders, "What thanksgiving can we return to God for you?" (1 Thess. 3:9 ESV). To the Romans, he is filled with thanks and longing to be with them (Rom. 1:8–12). He tells the Ephesians that he does not cease to give thanks for them, remembering them in his prayers (Eph. 1:16).

Paul never shies away from praying with fervent fondness for his family in Christ. In the same way, our prayers for our children should overflow with thanksgiving. Of course, Paul didn't have to wake up at 3:00 a.m. to feed a screaming baby, break up the fourteenth fight of the day, or bear the cruel remarks of an angry teenager. I know Paul didn't have to do those things, but he loved all of these churches like they were his children. He did have to rebuke them and bear with them as they sinned against him and each other. These weren't model churches with perfect congregations; they were real churches made up of God's children, sinners in need of grace. Paul is trying to see them the way Christ saw them and love them the way he was loved. In the same way, we can ask the Holy Spirit to help us see our children like he does, with great hope and love. We can ask him to help us be "grace detectives"—to be more aware of how the Lord is working in their lives than in how they are failing. I'm trying to learn to start each of my prayers for them with words something like, "Lord, I thank you for Marcus. Please help me see where you're working in him. Thank you for sustaining his life. Thank you that he's not pretending to be a believer. Thank you that he's still in our home." Starting with thanksgiving reminds us of our love for our children and makes our hearts tender toward them.

After his time of thanksgiving for the people, Paul goes on to tell them of his prayer for them. He prays they would walk worthy of their calling, do good, and be filled with knowledge and wisdom. He prays the Lord would give them grace to love each other more and they would be restored to perfect fellowship with the Lord and with one another. These are the type of prayers I normally offer for our children: "Lord, please help Kenyon to be kind today and have self-control." We might pray for our children's salvation or for their future spouse, but typically I limit my prayers to the behaviors I see that affect the family most.

After these first two steps, Paul's prayers begin to differ from the way I normally pray. He does pray they would love each other, but always in light of the way they have been loved. He prays they would have knowledge and insight, but always a knowledge and insight about Christ's love for them. He prays they would know Jesus's power at work in them. Yes, he does pray they would do good, but not so that he would look good or because he's worked so hard for them. He prays they would respond in gratitude for Jesus Christ. He asks the Lord to help them become pure and blameless, but only in light of the fact that they are already called pure and blameless by God.

If we have children who don't yet believe, we should be fervently calling out to God, pleading they would see the riches and fullness of Christ's grace. Praying that every member of the family would believe in his grace should be our constant prayer. In that way, our prayers echo Paul's, asking that our children's eyes would be open to the glorious power of God, who created the heavens and yet intimately cares for their souls.

In every prayer, Paul exudes confidence in God's work in the churches. When we listen, we can hear him praying and believing his prayers have already borne fruit. This confidence doesn't come from his trust in his fellow saints; he's very well acquainted with their failures. Instead, his confidence comes from God. He knows that "by his power," the faithful Lord will care for them and guard them. He prays each person would be "strengthened with power through his Spirit" (Eph. 3:16 ESV), because "He who calls you is faithful; he will surely do it" (1 Thess. 5:24 ESV). Paul is confident in his prayers because he believes Christ's words on the cross. When Jesus uttered those three glorious words, "It is finished," it meant that "he who began a good work in you will carry it on to completion" (Phil. 1:6).

I'll admit that, at times, my prayers for my children are nothing more than vocalized unbelief aimed at God. Imagine my son is angry and has been unkind, hurting me and others for the past two hours. When he finally comes to me and asks for prayer, I can barely muster a "Lord, help him to stop crying and be nice." I pray this way because I am angry, and because I have forgotten who is at work here. I don't believe anything more than feigned repentance is happening. I doubt my son will ever change. So, when he asks me to pray, I do, but I don't have any thanksgiving or faith to see what the Lord is up to. I'm forgetting it is not my feeble attempts at parenting that are going to change this child but rather God at work in him.

Sometimes the Holy Spirit reminds me I can pray with confidence that my child will be changed, not because of my great prayer or my great parenting but because this is what God is working toward also. But in such moments of anger, I feel alone in my parenting. I feel helpless in my parenting. I feel utterly confused and weak in my parenting. But the truth is I am not alone; I have the Helper, and he is teaching me that I must have confidence in his strength, not my own. So, by faith I'm learning to rephrase my prayer. Instead of praying my son would "stop crying and be nice," I begin to thank God for him. I thank God he's been entrusted to our family. I thank God he has come to me for help and is beginning to believe prayer can make a difference. I do pray the Lord would help him love his siblings, and then I begin to remind both of us of what Jesus has already done for us. Jesus lived in a family with irritating siblings. They certainly were selfish and sinned against him. And yet he loved them. I remind myself and my dear son in prayer that this matters, because if he would believe it, this record of love can be his too. The Lord has beautifully transformed my heart, and instead of being focused on all that I am suffering, I am able to remember his sufferings and look to him for grace.

Parents can pray for their children with thanksgiving, purpose, and confidence. We can pray this way for ourselves also. In moments of weakness and desperation, when our children seem to have forgotten everything we've ever said, we can begin our communication with our Father by praying we would see what he's already done for us. We can be thankful for God's work in our children and in us. Once our hearts are settled in his great love for us, we can pray he would open our eyes to see how magnificent he is. He loves us and calls us his dear children! Because of his loving welcome, we can love our children and welcome them back into relationship with open arms. And they can learn to love too. Then, remembering he is "able to do far more abundantly than all that we ask or think, according to the power at work within us" (Eph. 3:20 ESV) will boost our faith to pray prayers that are simply mind-boggling. Can the Lord really save *that* child? Is he able to teach *them* about his love? Will *they* ever really come to know and believe it?

He Always Hears His Son's Prayer

Therefore, since we have a great high priest who has ascended into heaven, Jesus the Son of God, let us hold firmly to the faith we profess. For we do not have a high priest who is unable to empathize with our weaknesses, but we have one who has been tempted in

192

every way, just as we are—yet he did not sin. Let us then approach God's throne of grace with confidence, so that we may receive mercy and find grace to help us in our time of need. (Heb. 4:14–16)

Jesus Christ blazed a trail into heaven for us. He did this by sacrificing his blood, allowing his flesh to be torn so that the pathway into the Father's presence would forever be open to us. He annihilated every obstacle that would bar our entrance into the Holy of Holies where our prayer-answering Father dwells. From his first breath, he lived a life of perfect dependence on his Father, carrying on a continual conversation with him, giving thanks and submitting himself to the love and guidance of the Father. Jesus Christ always prayed without ceasing and always in accordance with his Father's will. He did this because he loved conversing with his Father but also so that our record before our Father would be one of perfect prayer and submission too. We don't need to pray to prove we're properly pious or really serious. Instead, we pray because we are completely assured the Father hears our prayers *because they come to him through the lips of his dear Son.* Can our prayers sometimes be weak, scrambled, inconsistent, or self-centered? Of course. Even so, we can take heart because the true cries of our hearts are always voiced by the beloved Son, our great high priest.

So, lean in to him. Don't be afraid you'll fail at this. Don't think he'll judge you because you don't say the right words with the right inflection and all the proper theology. Don't think he'll sniff at your requests because your family is such a mess. Be assured that these things will never happen for one simple reason: the record of our prayer has already been written. The Father hears the perfectly worded, properly believing, and flawlessly theologically correct prayers of his beloved Son when we pray.

We can freely pour out our hearts to our Father, knowing that Jesus, our dear Savior, will purify and transform our words into petitions that please him. When your prayer is freely spoken, joyful, and honest, your children will learn to pray like this too. Teach them that he is the High King of heaven, someone to respect and be in awe of, but also teach them that he is their dear Father—one who delights to hear their requests, even when they say them all wrong and don't have much faith and mumble them as a last resort. Go tell your Father about everything that's in your heart, and don't be afraid. The Lord Jesus is mediating for us all.

Remembering God's Grace

There isn't a right or wrong way to approach the throne of grace when it comes to praying for your children. As you reflect on what you've learned in this chapter, know you're not alone in this, your heavenly Father is with you and knows how to help you, and he'll answer you when you call.

1) How does believing the gospel change the way you think about prayer and how you pray?

2) How does the fact that the Son prays perfectly on your behalf encourage you in your prayer life?

3) What can you pray about for your children today?

11

Weak Parents and Their Strong Savior

I thought parenting was going to portray my strengths, never realizing that God had ordained it to reveal my weaknesses.

Dave Harvey[1]

I hate you, and I'm never coming back!"

The door slammed, and Aaron was gone. Jonathon and Karen broke down into tears . . . again. All they wanted was for Aaron, their son, to realize how much they loved him and desired what was best for him. But all Aaron could see was how controlling and strict his parents were compared to every other parent he knew. Both Aaron and his parents felt misunderstood, hurt, and angry. Aaron had threatened to leave so many times before, but his parents never really thought he would. How would they explain this to their church? Their family had long been lauded as exemplary. All their kids had been so well-behaved, polite, and kind. Jonathon and Karen had been told so many times by so many different people that they were great parents that they had started to make it their identity. But in the last year Aaron, their youngest, had decided it was time to rebel against everything they had taught him. They were totally befuddled by this. They had raised each of their children in exactly the same way. Why did the others turn out so good, and why did Aaron hate them so much?

"Lord, where are you? We thought you would bless our efforts. We've done everything we could do. We thought you would turn his heart toward you. Why is this happening? Where did we go wrong?"

Locked in the bathroom, Shelley couldn't believe what was happening. She could hear her kids screaming in the other room. Her twin boys were at it again, fighting over some toy they had played with a gazillion times. Why couldn't they just take turns? What happened to the timer she bought them so they wouldn't have this problem? She wanted to go into the living room, take all their toys, and throw them in the trash. But their fighting wasn't even what was troubling her the most at the moment. When going through her daughter's phone just now, she had found direct messages between her fourteen-year-old daughter and a sixteen-year-old boy at church. How could she have been so blind? She'd had no idea her daughter had two Instagram accounts. She only knew of the approved one she saw. The messages started out innocently enough, but had grown into something Shelley was embarrassed and angered to read. And not only had her daughter been lying to her, she had been stealing from her in order to buy little gifts for this boy. Shelley knew the boy from church, and he was not the type of boy she would ever want her daughter to talk to, let alone be "in love" with. The pain in the pit of her stomach kept getting stronger and stronger as she recalled the words emblazoned on the screen. Her daughter and this boy were supposed to meet today to "show each other how much they loved each other."

She wished she could go to her husband for help, but he was out of town—again. He wouldn't be home for two more days. And even when he was home, he never seemed as concerned as she was about the kids' behavior anyway. His typical response was, "They're kids . . . kids will be kids." Shelley sat on the bathroom floor and cried into a towel. When did her life take this horrible turn? She was faithful in attending church. She worked full-time just so her kids could go to a Christian school. She prayed for her kids almost daily. She had been the leader of the Moms In Prayer group at their school until last year, when she had to quit going because the pressures of working; driving to piano practice, baseball practice, and games; cleaning the house; and making dinner had just become too much for her. She had wanted to protect her daughter from the very situation that had gotten Shelley herself pregnant and married by the time she was nineteen. Was this God's way of punishing her? Should she have been more involved in their youth group, more involved in their school?

Parenting for the Glory of God

In the mid-1600s, godly men gathered together in London, England, for the express purpose of developing a teaching tool for training believers in the faith. This list of questions and answers is known today as the Westminster Shorter Catechism. The first question asked and answered is, "What is the chief end of man?" In modern jargon, we can rephrase this as, "What's the deal? Why are we here?" Their answer to this question of ultimate meaning has survived for centuries. *Why are we here?* The answer? "To glorify God and enjoy him forever." The definitive reason for our existence is to glorify God with our lives and enjoy him now and forever, throughout all eternity. Very simply, for us to glorify God means we recognize God's majesty in all things and make him appear as glorious as he already is through our words and our lives.

The vision for our lives as Christians is to glorify God like this through worship and obedience. We all hope to one day hear those blessed words, "Well done, good and faithful servant!" (Matt. 25:21). Every godly parent also earnestly hopes that their children will glorify the Lord, that they too will one day hear this "good and faithful" benediction. And although it is right and good to desire these things, the truth is none of us knows how God has ordained us to glorify him. The Lord has unique plans for each of his unique children in unique ways. Perhaps the way he's chosen for us to make much of him is through intense familial suffering. Perhaps it will be through sin and failure, maybe even through untimely death (John 21:19). Or maybe our parenting won't be a place of sadness or difficulty. If that is the case for you, accept that blessing from God.

Every believer is called to consciously seek to glorify God, but God isn't only glorified through our efforts, our victories, or our triumphs. He is glorified when we are sustained by his strength as we walk through the furnace of affliction and suffering. He is glorified when we receive and acknowledge his mercy and patience in our failures. Paul puts it this way: "For from him and through him and for him are all things. To him be the glory forever! Amen" (Rom. 11:36).[2] In other words, "Everything comes from him; Everything happens through him; Everything ends up in him. Always glory! Always praise!" (MSG).

Even through the strangest circumstances, God can show his glory. In Daniel 4:34–35, for example, we read that pompous King Nebuchadnezzar's insanity resulted in the praise of God's glory.

> Then I [Nebuchadnezzar] praised the Most High; I honored and glorified him who lives forever.
>
> > His dominion is an eternal dominion;
> > > his kingdom endures from generation to generation.
> > All the peoples of the earth
> > > are regarded as nothing.

> He does as he pleases
> with the powers of heaven
> and the peoples of the earth.
> No one can hold back his hand
> or say to him: "What have you done?"

The Lord Jesus holds all things together in himself and oversees everything—including our families.

> For in [Jesus] all things were created: things in heaven and on earth, visible and invisible, whether thrones or powers or rulers or authorities; all things have been created through him and for him. He is before all things, and in him all things hold together . . . so that in everything he might have the supremacy. (Col. 1:16–18)

As his children, we long to make his glory known by our faithful obedience. That is a good desire, but a strong, successful family may not be the way he has chosen for us to glorify him. Perhaps his goal is that we glorify him through our weaknesses and even failure.

The Strange Ways of God

This may be a very strange concept to you. As Americans, we generally can't wrap our minds around a success that seems like a failure. God's glory and our sins seem mutually exclusive. We treasure strength, not weakness; victory, not defeat; happy endings, not tragedies. But is that the message of the Bible? When we look closely at Scripture, do we see people who were always faithful, always strong and victorious, whose lives were shining models of virtue and faithfulness? Do we see heroes who left exemplary examples for us to follow? Or do we see something else in their lives?

And then we come to the paradigm-shattering, unfathomable gospel message. Here we see an insignificant, unwed pregnant girl, a midnight escape flight to Egypt, an itinerant preacher from a nowhere town who attracts a crowd of nobodies for a while and ends up deserted, shamed, and hanging exposed and bloody. In the end he is confounded by his Father's absence and seems to die in utter humiliation and defeat. How on earth can a story like that possibly ever bring the Creator of heaven and earth glory? Evil appears to have triumphed. Sin has been victorious. All is lost. God's glory might have been seen if Jesus had been able to get everyone to hail him as the beloved Son worthy of all praise and obedience. But this story? This weakness? How will his glory be seen now? Has sin really triumphed over God's desire to be glorified? No. *God's methods turn everything we assume about his glory upside down.*

> Our fall afforded Him the opportunity of showing that in the destruction of sin He could not only manifest His justice, but also glorify His mercy in remitting and forgiving sin, without infringing upon His righteousness. . . . Such is the edifice which the Almighty reared upon the ruins of sin.[3]

Our fall afforded him the opportunity of glorifying himself. In one monumental act of shocking grace, God demonstrated that he is mighty enough to transform what masquerades as utter defeat into great, God-glorifying victory. What an edifice he has "reared upon the ruins of [our] sin"! He uses our sin and failure to magnify his mercy, justice, and wisdom. And, make no mistake about it, the sins of Judas, Peter, Caiaphas, Pontius Pilate, the bloodthirsty guards, and the mindless masses were his instrument to glorify himself in a greater measure than he had ever been glorified before.

> Indeed Herod and Pontius Pilate met together with the Gentiles and the people of Israel in this city to conspire against your holy servant Jesus, whom you anointed. They did what *your power and will had decided beforehand should happen.* (Acts 4:27–28)

Because the Lord *always* acts for his own glory, and because he had predestined the sin of the Romans and the Jews in his Son's cruel execution, their sin glorified him. It was the means he used to demonstrate his grace, mercy, justice, and love so that we would sing his praises throughout eternity. Think about this: we would never know what mercy is if we had never sinned.

Now, before you throw this book across the room and accuse me of encouraging people to sin, please let me make a few things clear. I'm not encouraging anyone to sin. God hates sin. We all should hate it too. And because we never know what God's will is before it is accomplished, we must *always* assume that it is his will to be glorified by our obedience rather than our disobedience. We must continually strive *with all our might* for the "holiness without which no one will see the Lord" (Heb. 12:14 ESV). Further, just because God uses our failures for his glory, that doesn't negate the fact that if we are saved, Jesus had to suffer God's wrath for them. Sin is serious. It caused the Son to suffer.

I'm not telling you to sin. I'm telling you to strive against sin. I'm telling you to teach your children to strive against sin. But when the unexpected happens, when you and your children do sin, when you fail miserably, you need to know that God glorifies himself in your sin too. Everything God does is for his own glory, and he is completely sovereign over everything that occurs. He uses our sin and the sin of our children to glorify himself and to bring them to true freedom and lasting joy.[4]

Boasting in Weakness

Our modern worship of our personal success stories is clearly seen in the many parenting resources that focus on being successful parents who raise successful kids. It's the only paradigm we seem to be willing to accept. But what if we're measuring success in the wrong way? Could it be that our perception of success isn't God's plan for us or for our family? What if he's going to use our failures and our children's rebellion to make us humble comforters of other sufferers for his glory? What if he's called us to Jeremiah's seemingly unsuccessful ministry rather than Daniel's success? *Is there room in your parenting paradigm for weakness and failure, knowing that weakness and failure can glorify him?* These are difficult questions.

As we consider our children, it is our dearest prayer that they would seek to glorify him through genuine obedience and faith. Our hearts will break and we will weep if they do not. But don't we have to be willing to say that the chief end of our parenting is not our own glorification as great parents but rather to glorify God and enjoy him forever, *whatever* that means?

Not unlike most Bible characters, Paul's story isn't one of great worldly success. He would never have been counted as an influencer. In his sufferings and failures, Paul was taught the value of weakness by the Lord himself. For instance, at Damascus it was the Lord's will that he be forced to sneak out of the city in a basket under the cover of night, like a criminal. The great apostle Paul was a fugitive from the power of the religious elite and had to make himself very small and very quiet in order to escape persecution.

When Paul lists his ministry credentials, they don't include what we would call his accomplishments. No, instead he boasts about his weakness in things like afflictions, hardships, calamities, beatings, imprisonments, riots, labors, sleepless nights, and hunger (2 Cor. 6:4–5). Have you ever wondered if there was something lacking in Paul's interpersonal communication skills? Maybe he wasn't trying hard enough to get along with people; maybe he needed a book on how to have his best life now. Why would he have so much trouble if he was really serving the Lord?

Paul brags that he has the true marks of an apostle because he has "far greater labors, far more imprisonments, with countless beatings, and [was] often near death" (11:23 ESV). He was constantly in danger from rivers, in danger from bandits, in danger from my fellow Jews, in danger from Gentiles; in danger in the city, in danger in the country, in danger at sea; and in danger from false believers. I have labored and toiled and have often gone without sleep; I have known hunger and thirst and have often gone without food; I have been cold and naked. Besides everything else, I face daily the pressure of my concern for all the churches. (vv. 26–28)

What would we say to parents who had this degree of trouble in their parenting? Would we tell them they needed to get their parenting act together? Would we parade our children or our favorite parenting method before them? Would we assure them God wants them to overcome all their weaknesses so everything would run more smoothly? Paul was weak and subject to trials, just like us. *The obvious difference between Paul and us, though, is that Paul bragged about his weakness and we try to hide it.* We try to ignore it or fight against it. We think that Teflon-coated, spic-and-span, seamless parenting producing perfect little children all lined up like the Von Trapp Family Singers is the only thing that can possibly glorify God. *We're making him too small and our desires too big.*

At another time, after receiving a surpassingly great revelation from God, Paul was given a "thorn in [his] flesh" to keep him from becoming conceited about what he had seen. Imagine this: here is the great apostle with immense spiritual gifts who prayed prayers that serve as a model for us today. And yet the Lord refused to grant his request to remove this thorn (2 Cor. 12:7). *Three times.* Although we don't know what Paul's thorn was, we do know it was substantial. It's obvious that Paul was familiar with real suffering, but this thorn was far worse.

This thorn was ordained by God to keep Paul *humble and dependent.*

Paul also recognized that this thorn was "a messenger of Satan." Here's the astonishing truth: God used Satan to keep Paul from the sin of pride. Yes, we are to resist the onslaught of our enemy, and we are to pray that the Lord protects us from Satan's attacks on our family, but these attacks may be the very tool God will use in our lives to keep us from other sins like pride and self-reliance.

Your continuous struggles as a parent and your child's rebellion and hatred are painful, but through them is an opportunity to keep close to the Father. No one wants a thorn, as Paul experienced, especially when it happens within our parenting. None of us want to appear weak or incompetent or to have difficulties in our family. It can feel embarrassing and shameful when our parenting—good or bad—results in children who walk away from us or God. Yet we can grow in our faith when we believe the Lord will find a way through for our good and his glory. Has the Lord granted us the privilege of choosing how we'll glorify him? Would our chosen path *ever* lead us to the valley of the shadow of death with our children? If we spend our whole lives trying to avoid that valley, how will we ever experience the comfort of being sustained by his grace *in the valley*? The thorn becomes the place where Paul, the apostle who wrote more on grace than anyone else, needs grace. The weaknesses, failures, and sins of our families are the places where we learn that we need grace too. It is there, in those dark mercies, that God teaches us to be humbly dependent. It is there he draws near to us and sweetly reveals his grace. Paul's suffering teaches us to reinterpret our own thorn. Instead of seeing it as a curse, we are to see it as the very thing that keeps us "pinned close to the Lord."[5]

All-Sufficient Grace

Here are more precious words from Paul, our suffering brother, after he was denied his prayer request to be freed from his humiliating thorn:

But [the Lord] said to me, "My grace is sufficient for you, for my power is made perfect in weakness." Therefore I will boast all the more gladly about my weaknesses, so that Christ's power may rest on me. (v. 9)

Paul understands that personal success and strength are *barriers* to experiencing God's grace. God's sustaining power is seen and developed in our weakness and failure. The power of Christ flows through parents who boast in and embrace their personal weakness, not those who think they don't need it. Of course, every one of us will quickly confess that we know we need the power of Christ. Yes, yes, of course we do. But the veracity of our confident confession will be tested in our response to our weakness and failures—and to the weakness, failure, and sin of our children. Do we see these trials as God's gift to us? Do we see our children's struggles as our Savior approaching us in love to make his grace strong in our lives? Do we believe these trials open us up to Christ's grace?

While knowing the truth that God is with us in our trials doesn't take away the pain of the trial, we can hold both our pain and our confidence in him together. Like the psalmist, we can lament and be angry about our circumstances, but we ultimately trust in the wisdom of our loving Father (see Ps. 13). We won't do this perfectly, we won't do this consistently, but we can know that even in our distrust he is faithful to keep and guide us.

Whether we like it or not, whether we understand it or not, it is kind of the Lord to demolish our confidence in our own strength, abilities, and cherished methods. True, it doesn't feel kind at the time. It's terribly painful to watch your son turn from the faith or to hear that your daughter has been disruptive in Sunday school again. It crushes our hearts when we try and try to explain the gospel to our little ones and they stare back at us in boredom and resentment. Yet it is a kindness when he strips us of self-reliance because it is there, in our emptiness and brokenness, that we experience the privilege of his sustaining grace. It is only when we arrive at that dreaded place of weakness that we discover the surpassing power of Christ. It is only when we are finally freed from those oh-so-constricting straitjackets of self-righteousness that we are able to experience the true comfort and warmth of the robes of his righteousness.

His Power, Our Weakness

Our weakness is the place where we learn to depend on God's power. When we're stripped of everything we thought we could trust in, when we're absolutely desperate for help, the Lord moves into our circumstance and demonstrates his power. Sometimes he shows us his power by changing the circumstance, miraculously accomplishing what we never could. At other times he shows us how his sustaining grace enables us to endure situations that should crush us. Sometimes he makes us feel his strengthening arm upholding us in the trial. Other times he teaches us to walk by faith, believing his arm is there even though we don't feel it. It is in these varied circumstances that we learn of his greatness, his sustaining grace, and his ability to glorify himself in ways we would never have imagined.

We think compliant children will best teach us about his grace and the gospel, and they can. Compliant, believing children are frequently reflections of his great kindness. But the Lord also teaches us of his grace and the gospel through difficult children. We learn what it is like to love like he loved. We learn how to walk in his footsteps, and it is there, in our own personal upper room, where we learn how to wash the feet of those who are betraying us. It is there, kneeling before our rebellious children, that the real power of God is demonstrated. The compliant child's life fools us, assuring us that they are good because we're such good parents. The difficult children tell us the truth: God loves those who resist him, and he can infuse us with grace that will make us lay down our lives for them too. Their rebellion is a verification of the gospel. We produce sinful children because we are sinners, but God loves sinners. God's power is displayed through our failures when we tether ourselves to the gospel message of sin and forgiveness, no matter how desperate the situation becomes.

Content for the Sake of Christ

> For the sake of Christ, then, I am content with weaknesses, insults, hardships, persecutions, and calamities. For when I am weak, then I am strong. (2 Cor. 12:10 ESV)

Paul encourages us to move past simply putting up with our difficulties to being content in them. "Content" here doesn't mean Paul merely disciplines himself to respond with stoic apathy: "Oh well, I guess it's for the best . . . God knows . . ." No, the word Paul uses here, *eudokeō*, is so much richer, so much more colorful than that. It means he "takes pleasure in" or "approves" of these things.[6] Paul doesn't simply boast about his weaknesses; no, they please him. In fact, this word translated as "content" here is the same word the Father uses of the Son when he declares that he is "well pleased" with him (Matt. 3:17)! Paul's weaknesses, insults, hardships, persecutions, and calamities—by the mystery of grace—somehow left him at peace. Why? Why would Paul welcome weakness and calamity? Paul is content with these things for the "sake of Christ." This can be a hard word, but as Christ followers we can be held by the truth that ultimately his love will sustain us through everything.

Paul focuses his entire life on proclaiming one reality: Jesus Christ and him crucified. He doesn't have any other agenda, no other desire except that his life would display the glorious gospel message. He also believes God ruled sovereignly over every aspect of his life, so he sees every trial, every betrayal and desertion, and all his weakness as God giving him another opportunity to learn about him and rejoice in him before a watching world. That's how he can make statements like these:

> Christ will be exalted in my body, whether by life or by death. (Phil. 1:20)

> Prison and hardships are facing me. However, I consider my life worth nothing to me; my only aim is to finish the race and complete the task the Lord Jesus has given me—the task of testifying to the good news of God's grace. (Acts 20:23–24)

> I am ready not only to be bound, but also to die in Jerusalem for the name of the Lord Jesus. (Acts 21:12–13)

> For we who are alive are always being given over to death for Jesus' sake, so that his life may also be revealed in our mortal body. (2 Cor. 4:11)

> Now I rejoice in what I am suffering for you, and I fill up in my flesh what is still lacking in regard to Christ's afflictions, for the sake of his body, which is the church. (Col. 1:24)

In responding this way to his afflictions, Paul is following in the footsteps of his dear Savior, who confessed when facing the cross, "Now my soul is troubled, and what shall I say? 'Father, save me from this hour'? No, it was for this very reason I came to this hour. Father, glorify your name!" (John 12:27–28).

Father, Glorify Your Name

Are you willing to pray your Father would glorify his name in your life, in your children's lives, no matter what the cost? Are you willing to rest in every weakness and calamity if it means that the power of Christ rests on you and the Father is glorified? We know these are challenging questions. They challenge us too.

So we throw ourselves on the mercy of God and plead he will give us grace in every trial. We trust he will open our eyes to the joy that awaits us when all of the benefits of his life, death, and resurrection will be ours.

We accept that weakness and affliction are the milieu in which we now live. But it won't always be like this, because although Jesus was "crucified in weakness" he now "lives by God's power" (2 Cor. 13:4). The seeming triumph of our enemy over all that we love is not the end of our story. Has the Lord already triumphed victoriously over all our enemies? Yes! Will he bring all of his children safely home to him? Yes, of course! The pastor to the Hebrews assures us the Father has put everything in subjection to Jesus, leaving "nothing outside of his control" (Heb. 2:8 ESV). And yet, do we now see everything in his hands? No, but "we do see Jesus, who was made lower than the angels for a little while, now crowned with glory and honor because he suffered death" (v. 9). We admit we don't see everything coming together as we think it should for his glory right now. Not ourselves, our parenting, or our children seem to be completely submitted under his rule. But with the eyes of faith, we *can* see him.

> Though you have not seen him, you love him; and even though you do not see him now, you believe in him and are filled with an inexpressible and glorious joy, for you are receiving the end result of your faith, the salvation of your souls. (1 Pet. 1:8–9)

We can embrace our weakness and the difficulties of parenting because they are the means the Lord will use to acquaint us with the realities of his gracious power. But this weakness and affliction aren't all there is. Even now, we can be "filled with an inexpressible and glorious joy" (v. 8) because we believe he has saved our souls and will never forsake us in the work of parenting, and he is powerful enough to guide our children to himself.

So, go ahead. Commit to the work of being a parent who manages, nurtures, trains, and corrects your children in faith today. Teach them of God's precious promises that can transform their hearts. Pray for their salvation and that they would come to know and believe the love he has for them. But hold all your labors, all your prayers, all your plans *very loosely*. And make it your overriding desire that the Father would be glorified in every aspect of your life, whichever way he turns it. Perhaps his plan is for your family to be a wonderful example of his grace because you have such respectful, obedient children. Perhaps his plan won't look anything like that. But whatever his plan for you is, you can rest in the assurance that he will *always* strengthen you by his grace and for his glory.

Remembering God's Grace

Thank God we have a strong Savior when we are weak! Thus, we are never without hope in this journey of parenting. As you reflect on the following questions, let grace cover you and meet you in all your needs.

1) How can your weaknesses and failures glorify your heavenly Father?

_____

_____

2) How can you encourage yourself and your children when you encounter sin or weakness in your heart?

_____

_____

3) What would it look like to boast in your weakness, as Paul said? How would this change the way you view yourself and your children?

12

Resting in Grace

Therefore, there will be no rest for my bones or yours unless we listen to the Word of grace and stick to it consistently and faithfully.

Martin Luther[1]

It had already been a really hard morning. Conflict between Lindsey and her spouse was exacerbated by a combination of worry about changes at his job and the general chaos endemic to clothing and feeding seven people in their cramped 1½-bathroom house. In addition, it had started to snow overnight. The children would probably have to stay indoors for most of the day, and her plans to clean out the hall closet were going to have to be put on hold again. And now the two older boys were fighting again, her eldest was asleep on the couch *again*, and the toddler was crying because she'd spilled her juice all over her princess dress . . . *again*. Lindsey's head ached and she felt chilled, and she wondered if this was the beginning of another bout with the flu. *Give them grace? Ha!* Grace was the furthest thing from her mind. At this point,

213

she'd be happy to simply make it through the next fifteen minutes without giving way to her frustration and despair, let alone give her children anything else aside from well-deserved time-outs in different corners of the house. *When do I get my time-out? What I would give for fifteen minutes of peace and quiet in a corner!*

Does your heart resonate with Lindsey's story? No matter how disciplined, organized, and faithful we are, the reality is we are sinners living in a sin-cursed world with other sinners. Nothing we can do will ever change that. We're surrounded by the realities of "moth and rust [and] thieves" (Matt. 6:19 ESV)—Jesus's candid diagnosis of our condition. Yes, all things need to be made new, but we're not the ones who will accomplish that renovation (Rev. 21:3–5). We're exiles and strangers who see the promises from afar and believe them (Heb. 11:13), but we're walking by faith now, not by sight. Yes, a new day when everything will be made right will come, but in the meantime, while we're living in the *not yet*, we need grace. And not just a tiny bit; no, the truth is we're desperate for buckets of grace. We need it every hour of every day. We need it when we remember that we need it, and we need it when all we can see before us is futility and trouble and disappointment. We need grace. So, let's share some thoughts about grace together before we bring our time to an end.

Jessica and I know you want to give your children grace just the same way we do. We know you long to share God's story with them and watch his grace transform them. We know you love them and want what is best for them, and you're committed to doing the hard work he's called you to.

Responding to Grace

Perhaps some of you are really overjoyed about what you've read in this book and can already feel the load of guilt and fear sliding away. To know that the Lord loves us and uses us for his glory, and that he can save our children in spite of our parenting rather than because of it, may have been very good news to your burdened soul. God's grace has brought sweet refreshment for your dry faith, and now you're beginning to really rest in it. Sure, you know you don't get it all the time—and you know that's the point. You need a Savior, and you have one. Whew!

However, some of you only wish that what you've read here is true for you. *You mean I can stop doing and doing and doing and rest in God's grace and sovereignty alone? That sounds great, but I don't think I can let myself believe it. Because what about this . . . and what about that . . . and . . . ?* I (Elyse) know this is a common response because I've had this conversation with so many parents. They would like to believe they can relax and trust the Lord—if only they could be sure that they're being responsible enough. They have a thousand scenarios they want me to work through with them. *Yes, but what if she never prays? What if he doesn't ask for forgiveness? What if . . . ? What if . . . ?* Their love for their children, coupled with fear, makes them want a guaranteed method of handling every situation with complete certainty. They're serious about being godly parents, and they really don't want to give themselves a pass if resting in grace somehow means they aren't holding up their part of the bargain. They need grace to believe that, thankfully, there is no bargain. If there were, they would never be able to uphold their part of it, no matter how hard they try. No bargains, no meritorious works, just grace.

Recently I was having a conversation with a mom who was trying to wrestle through the implications of grace in her parenting methods and responsibilities. She admitted that she had read too many parenting books. She had exhausted herself trying to be a good mom and meet all the needs of all her children, raising them for the Lord. She had thought there was a bargain between her and God. So she homeschooled and baked bread and made their clothes. They avoided television. They only read books written in the 1800s. Now, in the middle of all her pain and exhaustion, she was trying to embrace grace but continued to be crippled by fear and guilt. "I wish I had never read those books," she admitted. "I feel guilty and exhausted all the time."

I asked her, "How would you raise your children if all you had was the Bible?"

"Well, I guess I would love them, discipline them, and tell them about Jesus."

I smiled. "Right."

Remembering the Gospel of Grace . . . Again

Jessica and I know that sometimes it is nearly impossible to re-member the gospel at all, let alone think about ways to bestow it on our children. *Jesus? The cross? What?* And then, when we find ourselves floundering without a clue, we're overcome with guilt because we're not living up to our own expectations. *I thought that understanding the gospel of grace and how it applies to parenting would transform me, but here I am forgetting what he's done and being the same old me . . . again!*

When we forget the gospel and then feel guilty about it, *we're completely missing the point of the gospel.* Our ultimate joy as parents is not dependent on our ability to parent well. God's smile on us is not contingent upon anything other than the record of his beloved Son. It is based on our belief that Jesus has already done it all perfectly for us. Grace simply means resting in Jesus's blood and righteousness.

If you resonated at all with the little scenario that opened this chapter, you need grace too. Giving kids grace is not a new gim-mick, a secret key that will automatically unlock the door to a carefree and manageable life. It won't ensure your children will be godly, nor will it make your spouse instantly more helpful when the juice cups topple. It's not something you will always remember, nor will you understand how it applies in every situation even when you do remember it. *Grace is God's favor given to you because of Jesus Christ, not because of your consistent memory of it.*

Grace is not a "thing." It is not a substance that can be measured or a commodity to be distributed. It is the "grace of the Lord Jesus Christ" (2 Cor. 13:14). In essence, it is Jesus himself.[2]

Grace is demonstrated in the life, death, resurrection, and ascension of Jesus Christ, accomplished for you. It is all that he was, is, and ever will be. He loved perfectly in your place. He obeyed consistently. He always remembered. He now lives as your faithful elder brother and high priest interceding for you. Jesus Christ himself is God's grace to you. He is the door that opens up access to your loving Father's heart. Grace is what he has given to you: it is that oh-so-costly unmerited favor. And with that favor comes his strength to persevere through every trial of parenting. Grace is not a novel, fail-safe catchphrase that will ensure successful parenting. No, it's something so much better than that! It is God's assured favorable attitude toward undeserving rebels whom he has, in his inscrutable love, decided to bless!

When he looks with favor upon us as beloved children, he also supplies the strength or grace we need to persevere through every trial of life, whether we remember his grace or not. Grace isn't created by our ability to work at it or even remember it—that's why it's called *grace*. Paul makes this point abundantly clear when writing about his saved Jewish kinsfolk who were "chosen by grace. But if it is by grace, it is no longer on the basis of works; otherwise grace would no longer be grace" (Rom. 11:5–6 ESV). Parenting in grace is not parenting on the basis of our own consistent gospel-centeredness. It is just the opposite. Parenting in grace is parenting on the basis of Christ's consistent perfections *alone*.

Growing in Grace

None of us, not even Jessica and I, know everything we will one day know about grace. We, too, frequently forget the gospel and quickly slip back into methods of parenting that are driven by anything but the gospel. But we're not alone in our deficiency in understanding and apprehending grace, which is why Peter wrote these words about grace that function as bookends to his second letter.

Grace and peace be yours in abundance through the knowledge of God and of Jesus our Lord. (2 Pet. 1:2)

But grow in the grace and knowledge of our Lord and Savior Jesus Christ. To him be glory both now and forever! Amen. (3:18)

Can we see how growing in grace is in some ways synonymous with growing in our knowledge of the gospel? In other words, the more time we spend pondering what Jesus has already done for us, the more we will comprehend grace—how favored we are because of what Jesus has done. And this understanding will eventually transform how we parent our children. We will favor them with our love and attention because we'll see how we have been so abundantly favored. We'll be conscious of our sin when we see theirs, and we'll stop trying to preserve our great reputation as parents. We'll be patient because God's been so patient with us. We'll really love because we've been really loved. This understanding of the foundation of grace will *slowly* transform our expectations, hopes, and desires for ourselves and our children. Grace changes everything about us . . . even when we forget it.

Grace transforms our parenting because it makes our sin immense in our own eyes by showing us the hideousness of the bloody cross that was necessary before God could favor us with forgiveness. At that cross, every sin we've committed as parents was placed upon Jesus. Grace makes mercy huge because it reveals the price he had to pay to bestow it on us. We deserved judgment, but we've been given mercy! God's great mercies are magnified because we see the unimaginable suffering of the Son who fulfilled all righteousness and was forsaken (Matt. 3:15; 27:46).

Grace magnifies Jesus Christ and shows us our weakness and dependency.

So, when we have that morning to top all mornings, when everything that could possibly go wrong does, when grace doesn't mean anything to us, it is his grace that will sustain us. What mornings like these teach us is that we're just like our children. They forget and so do we. They need grace and so do we. We're partners in grace with them.

Humble Partners in Grace

When we're feeling our weakest, and we really don't have any idea how grace or the gospel might apply in our current situation (and are not sure if we care), we'll know that it's okay to be silent and simply wait. Many times our children don't understand the gospel or grace either. We don't need to try to drum up some gospel speech that isn't resonating within our hearts every time they disobey to be sure we've got our bases covered. We're partners with our children because we're just like them—dearly loved sinners. It will comfort their souls when they see there isn't something intrinsically wrong with them because they don't understand the gospel all the time.

Conversely, when we get so wrapped up in whether we're saying the right thing at the right time and trying to see into their hearts to be sure there is some sort of faith or change happening that we become afraid of making mistakes, that is when we fall back into self-reliance. When we think everything is up to us, we won't see how we're to partner with our children as beloved fellow-sinners. Instead, we'll mistakenly assume it's up to us to make them believe and change their hearts. We can't get at their hearts. We can't even get at our own (Jer. 17:9).

Partnering in grace with our children means we're learning to rely on the Holy Spirit together. Telling our children that we, too, are struggling to understand how the gospel would change us, and admitting we really don't see how it does right now, will teach them that faith doesn't mean having certainty or clarity all the time. Sometimes we'll simply need to manage them while we wait for light. It's at times like this that we can honestly tell our children we're trying to see what the gospel looks like, and we're walking in shadow.

This place of transparency and brokenness before our children and the Lord will ultimately be a place of freedom and grace, even though at first it will feel like a place of despair and humiliation. When we reach a real understanding that there is nothing we can say or do that will change our children's hearts, at that moment we're in the place of humility that is the *only* door to promised grace.

All of you, clothe yourselves with humility toward one another, because,

> "God opposes the proud
> but shows favor to the humble."

Humble yourselves, therefore, under God's mighty hand, that he may lift you up in due time. Cast all your anxiety on him because he cares for you.

Be alert and of sober mind. Your enemy the devil prowls around like a roaring lion looking for someone to devour. Resist him, standing firm in the faith, because you know that the family of believers throughout the world is undergoing the same kind of sufferings.

And the God of all grace, who called you to his eternal glory in Christ, after you have suffered a little while, will himself restore you and make you strong, firm and steadfast. To him be the power for ever and ever. Amen. (1 Pet. 5:5–11)

Although God has promised to resist parents who proudly assume they can save the day by their own efforts, he has also promised to give grace to those who humbly bow before him, casting all their cares on him and admitting their weaknesses and poverty. Only humility, only transparent confession of our great need will result in the grace we so desperately need to parent our children. We won't always be able to love them like we should. And there will be times we don't consistently raise them in the nurture and admonition of the Lord. Our job is not just hard, *it's impossible.* It is at those moments when we're struck dumb by our own failure and unbelief and brokenly fall on our knees before him that his promised grace is most powerful in us.

When we're feeling total despair, when we think, *I'm never going to get this right, and even when I try I fail,* it will be then, at that moment, that we'll have the grace to resist our enemy and watch how our Savior restores, confirms, strengthens, and establishes us. We need days of failure because they help humble us, and through them we can see how God's grace is poured out on the humble. It is on days like these that the words "who called you to his eternal glory in Christ" (v. 10) will bring deep comfort and great joy to your soul.

> *Oh, Lord, I can't see you now, and I feel so weak and inadequate, but you've promised that we'll be together in your eternal glory in Christ. Lord Jesus, I thank you and humble myself before you. Please help me see and believe.*

It is in times of humility, of saying that we're in great need, that his grace is promised to us. Do you feel the need for more grace to love your children and see the gospel in your daily life with them? Then rest in his arms and admit your brokenness. He's promised, and he's always faithful to keep his promises.

Leading Kids to Joy and Freedom

The one thing our children really need is the gospel of grace because that will lead them to experience the joy and freedom grace offers them. In experiencing the love, forgiveness, and blessings God gives abundantly through our parenting, they will experience the abundant life that is promised in Christ.

Living and parenting in grace is not the easy road. In fact, it is much harder to rest in God's promise of grace than it is to make a list and try to live by it. Some people may think that giving grace to your children equates to giving yourself a pass. Just the opposite is true. Giving grace to children is an exercise of faith, and faith is always more difficult than works. It flows out of humility, a character trait none of us comes by naturally. That's why most people miss it and why faith, not works, is the stumbling block of the cross. You're not slacking off when you tell your children of his never-ending grace and love. You're doing the hardest thing.

So, go ahead and give your kids grace when they succeed or fail. Show them how much he loves his little children. Bring them to him and encourage them to jump up on his lap and share all of their silly stories and fears and joys with him. Assure them of his great delight in them. And when they sin, when they fail, tell them the One Good Story all over again—grace, grace, amazing grace.

Go ahead and give yourself grace too. Whether you feel like a success or a failure, remember you are loved by your heavenly Father. He invites you to live into the joy and freedom his grace affords.

Remembering God's Grace

We've come a long way together. Hopefully you are finding new joy and freedom in the grace God has shown to you. As we finish our time together, take a few moments to prayerfully consider how the Lord has used this book to help you.

1) How does the grace God has shown you completely change the way you parent?

_____

_____

2) How does remembering God's grace help you in your failures as you parent?

_____

_____

3) How does remembering God's grace help you see your successes as you parent?

_____

_____

4) How can you now partner with your child in the gospel?

_____

_____

Acknowledgments

A book like this is a compilation of years and years of conversations in our communities. For that, we're so grateful.

We're thankful for all the parents who have encouraged and sharpened us along with way. We've heard from many of you since the original release of this book, and we hope this revised edition demonstrates that we've listened to the enlightenment and correction you've brought to us. Thank you for expanding our understanding of the good news and helping us appreciate the distinction between the rules and the gospel message. What an inheritance!

We're thankful for our agent, Don Gates, and his diligent help in representing us to Revell, and, of course, to our dear friend and editor, Grace P. Cho. Thank you for believing that this message is still necessary and for your eye to help us see from a new perspective.

I (Elyse) am thankful for the woman my daughter Jessica has become and for the deep spiritual insight and love for the Lord she lives out every day. I'm also incredibly thankful for all my children and their children—I am truly blessed. And of course, for dear Phil, who is always there, cheering me on. He's the truest example of the love of Jesus I have. Always yours, dear.

I (Jessica) wish I could express the magnitude of my gratitude to my children. You all have been the ones who have taught me grace in the ways you've loved me when I have failed you, in the ways you've laughed with me and at me, and in the ways you support me and cheer me on, even if we don't agree. I love being your mom, and I love being your friend. Thank you for loving me. To my Risen family, thank you for giving me the space to work on this. To my mom and dad, I have no idea where I would be without you.

The Best News Ever

I (Elyse) didn't begin to understand the gospel until the summer before my twenty-first birthday. Although I had attended church from time to time in my childhood, I'll admit that it never really transformed me in any significant way. I was frequently taken to Sunday school, where I heard stories about Jesus. I knew, without really understanding, the importance of Christmas and Easter. I remember looking at the beautiful stained-glass windows, with their cranberry red and deep cerulean blue and their picture of Jesus knocking on a garden door, and having a vague sense that being religious was good. But I didn't have the foggiest idea about the gospel.

When adolescence came barging in, my strongest memories are those of despair and anger. I was consistently in trouble, and I hated everyone who pointed that out. There were nights when I prayed that I would be good, or more specifically, that I would get out of whatever trouble I was in and do better. But then I would be disappointed and angered by the failures of the following day.

Upon graduation from high school at seventeen, I was married, had a baby, and was divorced before my nineteenth birthday.

During the following months and years I discovered the anesthetizing effects of drugs, alcohol, and illicit relationships. Although I was known as a girl who liked to party, I was utterly lost and joyless—and soon I began to recognize it.

I can remember telling a friend one day that I felt like I was fifty years old, which was the oldest I could imagine anyone being. I was exhausted and disgusted with myself, so I decided to set about improving myself. I started working a full-time job, took on a full course load at a local junior college, and cared for my son. I changed my living arrangements and tried to start over. I didn't know the Holy Spirit was working in my heart, calling me to the Son. I just knew that something had to change. Don't get me wrong; I was still living a shamefully wicked life, it's just that I felt like I was beginning to wake up to something different.

At this point, Julie entered my life. She was my next-door neighbor, and she was a Christian. She was kind to me, and we became fast friends. She had a quality of life about her that attracted me, and she was always talking to me about her Savior, Jesus. She let me know she was praying for me and would frequently encourage me to "get saved." Although I'd had that Sunday school training, what she had to say was something completely different from what I remembered ever hearing. She told me I needed to be "born again."

And so, on a warm night sometime in June 1971, I knelt down in my tiny apartment and told the Lord I wanted to be his. At that point, I didn't really understand much about the gospel, but I did understand this: I was desperate, and I believed the Lord would help me. That prayer on that night changed everything about me. I remember it so clearly, even now, as if it were yesterday.

In the words of Scripture, I knew I needed to be saved, and I trusted Jesus could save me. One man who came in contact with some of Jesus's first followers asked this same question: "What must I do to be saved?" The answer was simple: "Believe in the Lord Jesus, and you will be saved" (Acts 16:30–31).

Very simply, what do you need to believe in order to be a Christian? You need to know that you need salvation, help, or deliverance. You must not try to reform yourself or decide you're going to become a moral person so that God will be impressed. You just can't do it. Because he is completely holy—that is, perfectly moral—you have to give up any idea you can make yourself good enough to meet his standard. This is the *good* bad news. It's bad news because it tells you that you're in an impossible situation you cannot change. But it's also good news because it will free you from endless cycles of self-improvement that end in ultimate failure.

You also need to trust that what you're unable to do—live a perfectly holy life—he's done for you. This is the *good* good news. This is the gospel. Basically, the gospel is the story of how God looked down through the corridors of time and set his love on his people. At a specific point in time, he sent his Son into the world to become fully like us. This is the story you hear about at Christmas. This baby, Jesus Christ, grew to be a man, and after thirty years of obscurity he began to show the people who he was. He did this by performing miracles, healing the sick, and raising the dead. He also demonstrated his deity by teaching people what God required of them and continually foretelling his coming death and resurrection. And he did one more thing: he claimed to be God.

Because of Jesus's claim to be God, the leading religious people, along with the political powers of the day, passed an unjust sentence of death upon him. Although he had never done anything wrong, he was beaten, mocked, and shamefully executed. He died.

Even though it looked like he had failed, the truth is this was God's plan from the very beginning.

Jesus's body was taken down from the cross and laid hastily in a rock tomb in a garden. On the third day, some of his followers went to go properly care for his remains and discovered he had risen from the dead. They actually spoke with him, touched him, and ate with him. This is the story we celebrate at Easter. After another forty days, he was taken back up into heaven, still in his physical form, and his followers were told that he would return to earth in just the same way.

I told you there were two things you needed to know and believe. The first is that you need more significant help than you or any other merely human person could ever supply. The second is that you choose to believe Jesus Christ is the only one who can and will supply that help, and if you come to him, he will not turn his back on you. You don't need to understand much more than that, and if you really believe these truths, your life will be transformed by his love.

Below I've written out some verses from the Bible for you. As you read them, you can talk to God just as though he were sitting right by you (because his presence is everywhere!) and ask him for help to understand. Receiving help isn't based on your ability to perfectly comprehend or do anything. If you trust him, he's promised to help you, and that's all you need to know for now.

For all have sinned and fall short of the glory of God. (Rom. 3:23)

For the wages of sin is death, but the gift of God is eternal life in Christ Jesus our Lord. (6:23)

You see, at just the right time, when we were still powerless, Christ died for the ungodly. Very rarely will anyone die for a righteous person, though for a good person someone might possibly dare to die. But God demonstrates his own love for us in this: While we were still sinners, Christ died for us. (5:6–8)

God made him who had no sin to be sin for us, so that in him we might become the righteousness of God. (2 Cor. 5:21)

If you declare with your mouth, "Jesus is Lord," and believe in your heart that God raised him from the dead, you will be saved. For it is with your heart that you believe and are justified, and it is with your mouth that you profess your faith and are saved. As Scripture says, "Anyone who believes in him will never be put to shame." For there is no difference between Jew and Gentile—the same Lord is Lord of all and richly blesses all who call on him, for, "Everyone who calls on the name of the Lord will be saved." (Rom. 10:9–13)

And whoever comes to me I will never drive away. (John 6:37)

Therefore, if anyone is in Christ, the new creation has come: The old has gone, the new is here! (2 Cor. 5:17)

Come to me, all you who are weary and burdened, and I will give you rest. Take my yoke upon you and learn from me, for I am gentle and humble in heart, and you will find rest for your souls. For my yoke is easy and my burden is light. (Matt. 11:28–30)

Therefore, there is now no condemnation for those who are in Christ Jesus. (Rom. 8:1)

If you'd like to, you might pray a prayer that goes something like this:

Dear God, I'll admit that I don't understand everything about this, but I do believe these two things: I need help, and you love me and want to help me. I confess that I have ignored you most of my life, except when I was in trouble or just wanted to feel good about myself. I know I haven't loved you or my neighbor, and I recognize that I need your help to do so. But I also believe you've brought me here, right now, to read this page because you are willing to help me, and if I ask you for help, you won't send me away empty-handed. I'm beginning to understand how you punished your Son in my place and how, because of his sacrifice for me, I can have a relationship with you.

Father, please guide me to a good church community and help me understand your Word. I receive your grace and

*your love, and I commit to live this life with you. Thank
you for seeing me and loving me and calling me your child.
In Jesus's name, Amen.*

Here are two more thoughts. First, in his kindness, Jesus established his church to encourage and help each other understand
and live out these two truths. If you know you need help and
think Jesus is able to supply that help, or if you're still questioning
but want to know more, please search out a good church in your
neighborhood through the recommendations of trusted believers
or an internet search, and begin to create relationships there. A
good church is one that recognizes we cannot save ourselves by our
own goodness and that relies wholly on Jesus Christ (and no one
else) for this salvation. Each church has its own culture and values
outside of the basic statement of beliefs, so finding a good church
is sometimes quite a process. Don't be discouraged if you don't
succeed right away. Keep trying and believing God will help you.

Second, another factor that will help you grow in this new life
of faith is to begin to read what God says about himself and about
us in his Word, the Bible. In the New Testament (the last third or
so of the Bible), there are four Gospels or narratives about the life
of Jesus. I recommend starting with the first one, Matthew, and
then working your way through the other three. I also recommend
purchasing a good modern translation, like the New International
Version (NIV) or the Christian Standard Bible (CSB), but you can
get any version that you're comfortable with and begin reading
more of the Bible right away.

Thank you for taking time to read this little explanation of the
most important news you'll ever hear. You are so loved by God,
and his grace for you never ends.

Notes

Introduction

1. Julius J. Kim, "Rock of Ages: Exodus 17:1–7," in *Heralds of the King: Christ-Centered Sermons in the Tradition of Edmund P. Clowney*, edited by Dennis E. Johnson (Wheaton, IL: Crossway, 2009), 88.

2. Michael S. Horton, "Joel Osteen and the Glory Story," Westminster Seminary California, October 1, 2007, https://wscal.edu/resource-center/joel-osteen -and-the-glory-story.

3. Sally Lloyd-Jones, *The Jesus Storybook Bible: Every Story Whispers His Name* (Grand Rapids: Zonderkidz, 2007), 14–17. Emphasis added.

Chapter 1 From Teaching Rules to Giving Grace

1. We were first introduced to categories like these in Martin Luther's discourse on Galatians. Although the categories we've chosen are a bit different from his, we gleaned the idea of lower levels of law and obedience from his thought. See Martin Luther, *Galatians*, Crossway Classic Commentaries series, edited by Alister McGrath (Wheaton, IL: Crossway Books, 1998).

2. As quoted in Gerhard O. Forde, *On Being a Theologian of the Cross: Reflections on Luther's Heidelberg Disputation* (Grand Rapids: Eerdmans, 1997), 23.

Chapter 2 How the Gospel Makes Our Kids Good

1. Lloyd-Jones, *Jesus Storybook Bible*, 20.

2. Common grace is "God's genuine affection [that] has been poured out upon all persons regardless of who they are or what wrongs they may have done. As Jesus said, God 'causes his sun to rise on the evil and the good, and sends rain on the righteous and the unrighteous' (Matt. 5:45)." James Montgomery Boice, "Common Grace," Lambert Dolphin's Place, accessed January 9, 2024, http:// ldolphin.org/common.html.

3. "Heidelberg Catechism, Question and Answer 60," Christian Reformed Church of North America, accessed January 23, 2024, https://www.crcna.org /welcome/beliefs/confessions/heidelberg-catechism.

4. "For truly in this city there were gathered together against your holy servant Jesus, whom you anointed, both Herod and Pontius Pilate, along with the

Gentiles and the peoples of Israel, to do whatever your hand and your plan had predestined to take place" (Acts 4:27–28 ESV).

Chapter 3 Raising Our Kids by Faith and Grace Alone

1. As quoted in Forde, *On Being a Theologian of the Cross*, 127.
2. As quoted in Forde, *On Being a Theologian of the Cross*, 127.

Chapter 4 Jesus Loves All His Little Prodigals and Pharisees

1. Forde, *On Being a Theologian of the Cross*, 27.
2. "Jesus Loves Me, This I Know," lyrics by Anna Bartlett Warner (1859), tune by William Batchelder Bradbury (1862). Public domain.
3. "My Hope Is Built on Nothing Less," lyrics by Edward Mote (1834). Public domain.

Chapter 5 Grace That Trains and Nurtures

1. Bryan Chapell, *Holiness by Grace: Delighting in the Joy That Is Our Strength* (Wheaton, IL: Crossway, 2001), 126.
2. Chapell, *Holiness by Grace*, 126.
3. In the Colossians passage, Paul begins his instruction to families in this way: "And whatever you do, in word or deed, do everything *in the name of the Lord Jesus*, giving thanks to God the Father through him. Wives, submit to your husbands, as is fitting *in the Lord*. . . . Children, obey your parents in everything, for this pleases the *Lord*. Fathers, do not provoke your children, lest they become discouraged" (Col. 3:17–22). The context for all familial relationships is "in the Lord."
4. Paul ordinarily uses *kurios* (translated "Lord" in our passage) of the Lord Jesus.
5. Johannes P. Louw and Eugene Albert Nida, eds., *Greek-English Lexicon of the New Testament: Based on Semantic Domains* (New York: United Bible Societies, 1996), 466.
6. Ceslas Spicq, *Theological Lexicon of the New Testament*, translated by James D. Ernest (Peabody, MA: Hendrickson, 1994), 548.
7. Along these same lines, in Galatians 4:2, Paul writes that a father assigns "guardians and managers" (ESV) to oversee the training of his underage heir.
8. See also 1 Corinthians 4:14, "I do not write these things to make you ashamed, but to admonish you as my beloved children" (ESV), and 1 Thessalonians 2:11–12, "For you know how, like a father with his children, we exhorted each one of you and encouraged you and charged you to walk in a manner worthy of God, who calls you into his own kingdom and glory" (ESV).

Chapter 6 Wisdom Greater Than Solomon's

1. Edmund P. Clowney, *Preaching Christ in All of Scripture* (Wheaton, IL: Crossway, 2003), 147.
2. Clowney, *Preaching Christ*, 32.
3. Dennis E. Johnson, *Heralds of the King: Christ-Centered Sermons in the Tradition of Edmund P. Clowney* (Wheaton, IL: Crossway, 2009), 28.

4. Lloyd-Jones, *Jesus Storybook Bible*.
5. Emilie Le Beau Lucchesi, "Is Disciplinary Spanking Effective? Here's How It Can Affect the Brain," *Discover*, July 18, 2023, https://www.discovermagazine.com/mind/is-disciplinary-spanking-effective-heres-how-it-can-affect-the-brain; Brendan L. Smith, "The Case against Spanking," *Monitor* 43, no. 4 (April 2012): 60, https://www.apa.org/monitor/2012/04/spanking.
6. Of course, there are children who are settled in patterns of rebellion and defiance, no matter how much parents try to discipline them. You can find help especially geared toward these kinds of recalcitrant children in Elyse M. Fitzpatrick and Jim Newheiser, *When Good Kids Make Bad Choices* (Eugene, OR: Harvest House, 2005).
7. Luther, *Galatians*, 177.
8. Luther, *Galatians*, 148. Emphasis added.
9. Chapell, *Holiness by Grace*, 120.
10. Chapell, *Holiness by Grace*, 129.
11. See also Romans 8:12–17.
12. See Proverbs 1:8, 10, 15; 2:1; 3:1, 21; 4:10, 20; 5:1, 20; 6:1, 3, 20; 7:1; 19:27; 23:15, 19, 26; 24:13, 21; 27:11; 31:2.
13. Both father *and* mother are responsible to teach their children wisdom (Prov. 1:8; 6:20).

Chapter 7 The One Good Story to Guide All Parenting Decisions

1. See also Exod. 34:16; Neh. 13:1–3; and Ezra 9:2, which reads, "For they have taken some of their daughters to be wives for themselves and for their sons, so that the holy race has mixed itself with the peoples of the lands" (ESV).
2. Rahab the harlot and Ruth the Moabitess are perfect examples of gracious redemption and intermarriage between former pagans and Israelites. There are other examples of the folly of intermarriage between believers and idolaters, such as between Solomon and his pagan wives (1 Kings 11:4).
3. Frank S. Thielman, "Notes on 1 Corinthians 7:14," ESV Study Bible (Wheaton, IL: Crossway, 2008), 2200.
4. Paul also commands those who were yet to be married to do so "only in the Lord" (1 Cor. 7:39 ESV). I've done enough counseling of women who married unbelievers and suffered significant struggles because of it to know that failure to obey in this area occasions great heartache.
5. "[Unequally yoked with unbelievers] is thus an image for being allied or identified wrongly with unbelievers. In context, it refers especially to those who are still rebelling against Paul *within* the church, whom Paul now shockingly labels as unbelievers." Scott J. Hafemann, "Notes on 2 Corinthians 6:14," ESV Study Bible, 2231. Emphasis added.

Chapter 8 Grace When It Comes to Anxiety and Depression

1. "About Project Semicolon," Project Semicolon, accessed January 12, 2024, https://www.projectsemicolon.com/about-project-semicolon-organization/.
2. Omari Fleming, "Rady Children's Hospital Seeing 30% Spike in Children Experiencing Mental Health Crises," NBC 7 San Diego, August 22, 2023, https://www

.nbcsandiego.com/news/local/rady-childrens-hospital-seeing-30-spike-of-chil
dren-with-mental-health-crises/3290827/?.

3. Fleming, "Rady Children's Hospital."

4. "Mental Health: Burden," World Health Organization, accessed January 12, 2024, https://www.who.int/health-topics/mental-health#tab=tab_2.

5. Andrey Zheluk, Judith Anderson, and Sarah Dineen-Griffin, "Adolescent Anxiety and TikTok: An Exploratory Study," *Cureus* 14, no. 12 (December 14, 2022): e32530, https://www.ncbi.nlm.nih.gov/pmc/articles/PMC9840731.

6. Frank Bruni, "Excerpt: Frank Bruni's *Where You Go Is Not Who You'll Be*," *New York Times*, April 25, 2016, https://www.nytimes.com/2016/04/25/insider/excerpt-frank-brunis-where-you-go-is-not-who-youll-be.html.

7. Jay Atkinson, "How Parents Are Ruining Youth Sports," *Boston Globe*, May 4, 2014, https://www.bostonglobe.com/magazine/2014/05/03/how-parents-are-ruining-youth-sports/vbRln8qYXkrrNFJcsuvNyM/story.html.

8. "COVID-19 Pandemic Triggers 25% Increase in Prevalence of Anxiety and Depression Worldwide," World Health Organization, March 2, 2022, https://www.who.int/news/item/02-03-2022-covid-19-pandemic-triggers-25-increase-in-prevalence-of-anxiety-and-depression-worldwide.

9. Bob Smietana, "Mental Illness Remains Taboo Topic for Many Pastors," Lifeway Research, September 22, 2014, https://lifewayresearch.com/2014/mental-illness-remains-taboo-topic-for-many-pastors/.

10. Charlotte Getz and Stephanie Phillips, *Unmapped: The (Mostly) True Story of How Two Women Lost at Sea Found Their Way Home* (Charlottesville, VA: Mockingbird, 2018), 256.

Chapter 9 Raising Girls and Boys in Grace

1. Dorothy Sayers, *Are Women Human?: Astute and Witty Essays on the Role of Women in Society* (Grand Rapids: Eerdmans, 1971), 11.

2. This chapter is adapted from Elyse M. Fitzpatrick and Eric M. Schumacher, *Jesus and Gender: Living as Sisters and Brothers in Christ* (Bellingham, WA: Kirkdale, 2022), chapter 9.

3. *Paedo baptism* means being baptized as a baby. *Credo baptism* means being baptized only after coming to faith.

4. *Exvangelicals* is a term frequently used to refer to people who were once part of an evangelical church and have since left that tradition or perhaps even faith altogether.

5. Frederick William Danker, ed., *A Greek-English Lexicon of the New Testament and Other Early Christian Literature*, third edition (Chicago: University of Chicago Press, 2001), 434.

6. See Elyse M. Fitzpatrick and Eric M. Schumacher, *Worthy: Celebrating the Value of Women* (Minneapolis: Bethany, 2020), chapters 8–10.

7. See Rachel Joy Welcher, *Talking Back to Purity Culture: Rediscovering Faithful Christian Sexuality* (Downers Grove, IL: InterVarsity, 2020). In *When God Writes Your Love Story* by Eric Ludy and Leslie Ludy (Portland: Multnomah, 2009), we read about a young woman who "had made the mistake of giving [her boyfriend] her most precious gift—her virginity," 237.

8. See Coleen Sharp and Rachel Miller, "Spiritual Abuse Q&A with Adia Barkley," *Theology Gals* (podcast), April 18, 2021, https://player.fm/series/theology-gals-2599188/spiritual-abuse-qa-with-adia-barkley. Adia Barkley talks about her experiences growing up in a Family Integrated Church where her father/stepfather acted as her mediator and decided whether she was worthy to receive communion. See also Scot McKnight, "Patriarchy by Any Other Name Is Still Patriarchy," *Christianity Today*, August 4, 2020, https://www.christianitytoday.com/scot-mcknight/2020/august/patriarchy-by-any-other-name-is-still-patriarchy.html.

9. The commandment against murder includes proper care for our own bodies: "The duties required in the Sixth Commandment are, all careful studies, and lawful endeavors, to preserve the life of ourselves and others," "Westminster Larger Catechism: Answer 135," The Westminster Standard: Larger Catechism, accessed January 23, 2024, https://thewestminsterstandard.org/westminster-larger-catechism/#131.

10. See, for example, Preston Sprinkle, *Embodied: Transgender Identities, the Church and What the Bible Has to Say* (David C Cook: Colorado Springs, 2021); Mark A. Yarhouse, *Understanding Gender Dysphoria: Navigating Transgender Issues in a Changing Culture* (Downers Grove, IL: IVP Academic, 2015); Andrew Marin, *Us Versus Us: The Untold Story of Religion and the LGBT Community* (Colorado Springs: NavPress, 2016). See also Guiding Families, https://guidingfamilies.com/, an organization that helps families of children who struggle with LGBTQ issues and has resources including articles and a private Facebook group. It also has resources for pastors and church workers who want to minister to the LGBTQ community in their church.

11. "The brain-sex theory proposes that there are areas of the brain that are different between males and females" (Yarhouse, *Understanding Gender Dysphoria*, 67). The difference proposed by adherents to the brain-sex theory is that it is caused by a testosterone wash that occurs during fetal development after the genitalia have already developed. Very simply put, the theory proposes there has been a disconnect between the development of the genitals and the testosterone wash, causing some who are physically sexed in one way to be naturally scripted to more common male or female dispositions or behaviors. Although there does seem to be a difference between the typical male/female brain, these differences are not necessarily caused by brain sex but rather by a combination of neurological changes caused by many factors over time. "It seems as though other variables need to be in the mix, and it is difficult to say with great confidence what those are" (Yarhouse, *Understanding Gender Dysphoria*, 79).

12. "63 percent of the kids . . . had one or more diagnoses of a psychiatric disorder or neuro-developmental disability preceding the onset of gender dysphoria." Sprinkle, *Embodied*, 163.

13. Sprinkle, *Embodied*, 141.

Chapter 10 Parenting through Prayer

1. Andrew Murray, *With Christ in the School of Prayer* (London: James Nisbet, 1887), 26.
2. Murray, *With Christ in the School of Prayer*, 43. Emphasis added.

3. Murray, *With Christ in the School of Prayer*, 25. Emphasis added.

4. Paul Miller, *A Praying Life: Connecting with God in a Distracting World* (Colorado Springs: NavPress, 2009), 59.

5. John Calvin, *John* vol. 1, Calvin's Bible Commentaries series (London: Forgotten Books, 2007), 171.

Chapter 11 Weak Parents and Their Strong Savior

1. Dave Harvey, unpublished sermon notes. Used by permission. Other content in this chapter, especially the section about weakness and the apostle Paul, has been inspired by Dave Harvey.

2. See also Ps. 115:1; Rom. 16:27; Gal. 1:5; Eph. 3:21; 1 Tim. 1:17; 2 Tim. 4:17–18; Heb. 13:20–21; 2 Pet. 3:17; Jude 25; Rev. 1:5–6; 4:11; 5:11–13; 19:6–7. God used Paul's previous identity as Saul, the murderous persecutor of the church, to glorify himself:

> The saying is trustworthy and deserving of full acceptance, that Christ Jesus came into the world to save sinners, of whom I am the foremost. But I received mercy *for this reason*, that in me, as the foremost, Jesus Christ might *display his perfect patience* as an example to those who were to believe in him for eternal life. To the King of ages, immortal, invisible, the only God, be honor and glory forever and ever. Amen." (1 Tim. 1:15–17 ESV)

How many times has your heart been encouraged by Peter's denial of the Lord and the Lord's welcome and restoration of him? God uses Peter's great sin to demonstrate what a great Savior he is.

3. F. W. Krummacher, *The Suffering Savior* (Carlisle, PA: Banner of Truth Trust, repr. 2004), 9–10.

4. Although God rules sovereignly over our sin, he is not responsible for it. We are responsible for our sin; he is not. And yet, there is a place where our sin and his sovereignty intersect for his glory. This intersection between our responsibility and his sovereignty is called *concurrence*.

5. Paul Barnett, *The Message of 2 Corinthians* (Downers Grove, IL: Inter-Varsity, 1988), 178.

6. Rick Brannan, ed., *Lexham Research Lexicon of the Greek New Testament* (Bellingham, WA: Lexham Press, 2020).

Chapter 12 Resting in Grace

1. Luther, *Galatians*, 33.

2. Sinclair Ferguson, *By Grace Alone* (Lake Mary, FL: Reformation Trust Publishing, 2010), xv.

ELYSE M. FITZPATRICK holds an MA in biblical counseling, is a frequent conference speaker, and is the author of over two dozen books. She's been married for nearly fifty years and has three children and six grandchildren who live near her in Southern California. She loves to proclaim the good news about the life, death, and resurrection of Jesus Christ, and how that glorious truth connects with our everyday lives.

JESSICA THOMPSON holds an MA in biblical studies. She has three adult children. She is on staff at Risen Church in San Diego, California. She has written several books about the love of Christ. You will find her living in the joy and freedom of the gospel while frequenting Padres games and Disneyland.